Reflective Writing for Language Teachers

Frameworks for Writing

Series Editor: Martha C. Pennington, Georgia Southern University

The *Frameworks for Writing* series offers books focused on writing and the teaching and learning of writing in educational and real-life contexts. The hallmark of the series is the application of approaches and techniques to writing and the teaching of writing that go beyond those of English literature to draw on and integrate writing with other disciplines, areas of knowledge, and contexts of everyday life. The series entertains proposals for textbooks as well as books for teachers, teacher educators, parents, and the general public. The list includes teacher reference books and student textbooks focused on innovative pedagogy aiming to prepare teachers and students for the challenges of the twenty-first century.

Published

The College Writing Toolkit: Tried and Tested Ideas for Teaching College Writing
Edited by Martha C. Pennington and Pauline Burton

The "Backwards" Research Guide for Writers: Using your Life for Reflection, Connection, and Inspiration
Sonya Huber

Exploring College Writing: Reading, Writing, and Researching across the Curriculum
Dan Melzer

Tend your Garden: Nurturing Motivation in Young Adolescent Writers
Mary Anna Kruch

Writing Poetry through the Eyes of Science: A Teacher's Guide to Scientific Literacy and Poetic Response
Nancy Gorrell with Erin Colfax

Reflective Writing for Language Teachers
Thomas S. C. Farrell

Forthcoming

Becoming a Teacher who Writes: Let Teaching be your Writing Muse
Nancy Gorrell

Writing from the Inside: The Power of Reflective Writing in the Classroom
Olivia Archibald and Maureen Hall

Arting, Writing, and Culture: Teaching to the 4th Power
Anna Sumida, Meleanna Meyer, and Miki Maeshiro

Seriously Creative Writing: Stylistic Strategies in Non-Fictional Writing
Sky Marsen

Welcome to My World: A Writing Course
Martha C. Pennington and Theresa Malphrus Welford

Reflective Writing for Language Teachers

Thomas S. C. Farrell

Published by Equinox Publishing Ltd.

UK: Unit S3, Kelham House, 3 Lancaster Street, Sheffield, S3 8AF
USA: ISD, 70 Enterprise Drive, Bristol, CT 06010

www.equinoxpub.com

First published 2013

ISBN 978-1-84553-536-0 (hardback)
978-1-84553-537-7 (paperback)

British Library Cataloguing-in-Publication Data

A catalogue record for this book is available from the British Library.

Library of Congress Cataloging-in-Publication Data

Farrell, Thomas S. C. (Thomas Sylvester Charles)
Reflective writing for language teachers / Thomas S.C. Farrell.
p. cm. -- (Frameworks for writing)
Includes bibliographical references and index.
ISBN 978-1-84553-536-0 -- ISBN 978-1-84553-537-7
1. Language and languages--Study and teaching. 2. English language--Rhetoric--Study and teaching. I. Title.
P53.F37 2012
418.0071--dc23

2011047766

Printed and bound in Great Britain by Lightning Source UK, Milton Keynes

Contents

Acknowledgments

This book reflects many of my experiences working with student-teachers, teachers, and colleagues over many years and in several different locations. None of the work would have been possible without my teaching experiences in Korea, Singapore, and Ireland, and I am forever grateful to all those I had the honor of working with and, of course, all of the students who gave me much to reflect on. To my teachers, Jerry Gebhard and Dan Tannacito, I offer my sincere thanks because of your encouragement to take on this topic in my dissertation, an uncommon topic at that time. I also would like to thank Jack Richards for trusting me to work with him on various projects over the years because this experience has been invaluable to me as an academic in the field from one who is at the top of this field. For keeping me reflecting while I was writing this book, sincere thanks go to Martha Pennington because she kept me on the straight and narrow throughout the project. Finally, to my ever suffering family who must endure my "reflections" as I write these books, many thanks to Mija, Sarah, and Ann.

Acknowledgements

Editor's Preface

Tom Farrell's *Reflective Writing for Language Teachers* asks teachers to consider their practice through the process and medium of writing. Farrell offers background and context on the nature and purpose of reflection, on the writing process, and on the value of reflection in helping teachers to see their work with new eyes and to advance themselves through self-directed professional development. He reviews different options for reflecting, such as teaching journals, narrative reflection, case studies, and action research. He offers guidance for group and pair reflection with a "critical friend" and for reflecting as a novice or more experienced teacher, along with examples drawn from language teaching contexts such as Korea and Singapore.

The author, a popular educator and workshop leader who is well known for his work in reflective teaching, has written a highly readable, engaging, and low-stress book that speaks right to the teacher and asks the right questions about teaching. Each chapter includes a wealth of questions and activities to guide the reader's reflective process, along with the author's honest reflections on his own personal journey towards becoming a reflective teacher and daily writer. In this book, Farrell successfully interweaves his personal narrative of becoming a reflective practitioner and writer with his insights and practical advice and activities for teachers to reflect on and write about their own work. Of particular interest is Farrell's personal story of how he became interested in applying reflection, which was the topic of his doctoral thesis, in his own work and then how he started writing to reflect on his own teaching.

Language teachers working in second language and foreign language contexts will find this a useful and enjoyable book that they can work through on their own or in a group of colleagues. Language teacher educators may also want to consider using this book with pre-service and in-service teachers to help them think about what they and other language teachers do and want to do in their classrooms. I predict that these different audiences will be drawn to the book by Farrell's highly accessible discussion of reflection, by his own modeling of the reflective process, and by the wide variety of probing questions he raises that are aimed to hit language teachers where they live, that is, in their classrooms and their professional lives more generally.

Martha C. Pennington
Series Editor, *Frameworks for Writing*

Introduction

Audience and Purpose

Reflective practice, in which teachers subject their beliefs and practices to critical reflection, is nowadays seen as a major component of many language teacher education and development programs world-wide. One method that has been suggested as to how language teachers can reflect on their work is by writing regularly about their practice. When language teachers write about various facets of their work over a period of time and then read over their entries looking for patterns, that is, seeing their own thoughts, they may uncover aspects of their practice that they had not realized before beginning to write reflectively. Reflective writing develops language teachers' understanding of their practice and can also lead over time to a clarification of the teachers' understanding of those beliefs and practices, and of the values and assumptions that underlie their practices. *Reflective Writing for Language Teachers* explores the impact of regular writing as a reflective tool for language teachers.

The primary audiences for this book comprise:

- Those taking graduate courses in ELL/ESL/EFL or Applied Linguistics who are interested in the field of second language learning and teaching;
- Teachers of languages other than English and those who work with these teachers;
- Classroom English language teachers who wish to further their professional development in in-service teacher development courses;
- Program administrators, supervisors, and teacher educators who are responsible for providing professional development opportunities for teachers.

Regardless of the context in which it is used, throughout the book I invite you to explore and examine your beliefs and understandings of language teaching and your knowledge and skills as you reflect on your own teaching. In what follows, I am not presenting prescriptions on how to reflect; rather, I am presenting ideas and modes of reflection that teachers can choose from to reflect at any time of their teaching day, or on other days when they are not teaching. Although writing is at the forefront of the reflective practice mode in the book, I acknowledge that other modes of reflection are also important (such as talking to and with other teachers).

Chapter Contents

Chapter 1, "Professional Development," outlines what professional development entails for language teachers and why teachers should engage in professional development at all stages of their careers. The chapter suggests that professional development often entails the realization by teachers that a change may be necessary in their professional lives, though they may not be sure how to go about changing or what change would mean for them. However, after they begin to learn how to *notice* various events in their professional lives, they can engage in more formal profe,ssional development activities as outlined in the chapter.

Chapter 2, "Reflective Practice," outlines and discusses reflective practice for language teachers and makes the case for language teachers to engage in reflective practice activities throughout their careers. The chapter defines reflective practice, overviews the different forms of reflective practice, and details various reflective practice activities that teachers can consider. These activities involve action research, teaching journals, concept mapping, teacher development groups, classroom observations, teacher metaphors, teacher maxims, teacher beliefs, and critical friendships.

Chapter 3, "Writing as Reflective Practice," outlines and discusses the different ways teachers can use writing as they reflect on their practice. The chapter distinguishes between writing as product and writing as process, and it explores how teachers can learn to write and also to revise their writing.

Chapter 4, "The Reflective Writing Journal," shows teachers how to focus their writing in journal formats as they reflect on their practice. The chapter outlines and discusses how teachers can use teaching journals to reflect and also outlines a case study of how one group of teachers used teaching journals to aid their reflections.

Chapter 5, "Narrative Reflective Writing," reminds teachers that they all have a story to tell about their work. The chapter explains what narrative writing is for language teachers and then shows how teachers can write their own narrative about their practice. The chapter also outlines and discusses how teachers can write and analyze critical incidents and case studies based on their own practice.

Chapter 6, “Reflecting in the First Year(s) and Beyond,” outlines and discusses how language teachers can begin reflections from their early days as novice teachers right into their years as experienced teachers. The chapter outlines the reflective process from student to teacher and then to experienced teacher. There is a special focus for novice teachers on reflecting in the early years because this is where the seeds of reflective practice are planted so that they can blossom in the later years.

Chapter 7, “Reflecting for Action,” outlines and discusses how language teachers can engage in reflective research throughout their careers. The chapter points out various ways teachers can engage in research as well as outlining one example from TESOL’s Language Teacher Research series.

1. Professional Development

Preamble

Ok! So you picked up this book and now you have opened it to the chapter on professional development. You are either an experienced teacher or a novice teacher, but regardless, you are curious enough to pick up the book and open this chapter. As this book is on the topic of reflective practice for teachers, and language teachers in particular, I will get straight into reflection by asking you to review and to try to write answers to the prompts of the first (of many) reflection journals that I hope get you in a reflective mood for the other chapters in this book. As you will see from this first reflection journal, you will be asked to write your answer first (after all, this book is about using writing as a tool to help you reflect) and then partner with one or more peers to consider your answers in relation to what others have written. Start by writing your initial reactions to the questions you read: you can write a reaction to each question, or be selective and respond to only one or two questions. Next, decide what you would like to share with a peer/colleague either orally or from what you have written. If you are reflecting for the first time and do not feel comfortable disclosing your reflections, you can just keep reflecting by yourself through writing as you go through the reflection journals in the book, you can ask a peer to join you later, or you can disclose just parts of your reflections. At this stage, your reflections are most important; that is why I ask you to write your reflections first, before discussing them, so that you can organize your thoughts as you write. As you write, do not worry about grammar, sentence organization, or spelling; simply write and continue to write whatever comes into your head. At this stage, the point is just to write and see what comes out.

I will introduce you to a phrase now that I will talk about more later in the book. Writing for me means that I can stop for a moment and slow down all of the different thoughts I have floating around in my head at the same time, to give some order and meaning to them. The phrase that helps me most to

Reflection Journal 1.1

First, write your own answers to these questions, and then find a partner or a group to discuss your findings and reflections; after these discussions in a pair or group, write a paragraph about your concluding reflections.

- What made you pick up this book, *Reflective Writing for Language Teachers*?
- Was it the title or something else?
- How did you react to the title of the book?
- How did you react to the table of contents of the book? Did any particular chapter topic interest you immediately, and if so, why?
- Did anything in the Introduction particularly catch your attention? If so, write about it now.
- How long have you been a language teacher?
- If you are a novice teacher, what do you think this book can offer you?
- If you are an experienced teacher, what do you think this book can offer you?
- Where did you learn most about teaching?
  - Own experience?
  - From others?
  - Experience as a learner?
  - Formal training?
  - Other?

do this is: *How do I know what I think until I see what I say?* You may find it helpful to keep this phrase in mind as a motivation for your reflective writing.

Teaching: Job or Profession?

Regardless of the context, in recent times, teachers are being encouraged and sometimes directed to engage in some kind of professional development throughout their careers so that they can continue to grow as teachers. Even before many novice teachers graduate from their teacher education programs, they are told that they will be required to sign up for development courses throughout their careers and that learning to teach is an ongoing, lifelong process. The obvious result of such early notice of this idea of ongoing professional development for novice teachers is that teachers may begin to wonder what they have learned in their teacher education courses and whether they have been sufficiently prepared for a career of teaching. Indeed, many administrators also wonder what novice teachers know when they come to their schools for the first time to teach because of all the professional development programs they will have to organize and fund throughout the school year. Many experienced teachers, too, wonder about all of the professional development mandates from the administration to keep up with new trends and theories in education throughout the school year. Many of these experienced teachers will see the new mandates, technology, curriculum, and methodology as merely the usual educational fads, which, as such, will disappear as quickly as they have been introduced. They have seen all this before: these professional development mandates are usually delivered by someone from the outside who knows nothing about their particular context, school, teachers, or students; and the someone, sometimes called an "expert," is often just pushing a new theory or

Reflection Journal 1.2

First, write your own answers to these questions, and then find a partner or a group to discuss your findings and reflections; after these discussions in a pair or group, write a paragraph about your concluding reflections.

- What does teaching mean to you?
- Do you think of teaching as a job or a profession?
- If you think teaching is a job, define your job.
- If you think teaching is a profession, define your profession.
- What have you done in the past year to develop yourself as a language teacher? [Check all that apply]
  - Attended workshops?
  - Attended talks/demonstrations by other teachers (e.g. brown bag lunches)?
  - Attended talks by invited speakers?
  - Attended short courses?
  - Attended in-service courses at your institution?
  - Attended conferences?
  - Worked with a colleague?
  - Observed other teachers?
  - Read language textbook teachers' manuals?
  - Read teacher resource books on teaching theory?
  - Read academic journals?
  - Read language teaching magazines?
  - Other?
- Where do you get ideas about teaching methods/techniques?
  - Talks/demonstrations by other teachers (brown bag lunches)?
  - Talks by invited speakers?
  - Workshops?
  - Short courses?
  - In-service courses at your institution?
  - Textbook teachers' manuals?
  - Conferences?
  - Teacher resource books on teaching theory?
  - Academic journals?
  - Teacher magazines?
  - Other?

book rather than really trying to help. Maybe you wonder whether this book might be just another in a long line of such "teaching fad" books?

Some teachers who have built up some years of experience may think that teaching is just a job and that they will mechanically "teach" students from 8:00 am to 2:00 pm each day without any real reflection on what they are doing. They just pick up the paycheck at the end of the month and enjoy the long summer vacations until they reach retirement and then receive their nice pension and thus live a cozy life. Why should they put any more effort into their work given that, after all, the students don't really care, the parents only look for problems, and the administration sees them as the costly part of their operating budgets? Why should they put any extra effort into the "job" of teaching, when school boards forced to make spending cuts always cut teachers first? Some teachers then get the idea that maybe they should just do their "jobs" and not care too much about the outcome, which is controlled by much more than they can influence in the classroom.

Develop as a Teacher! Who, Me?

It is a question then as to whether you should try to develop yourself as a teacher and if so, why you should. You may think you know all there is to know about your work, considering that you are a well-qualified and skilled teacher with lots of teaching experience. Another aspect of life as a language teacher, whether teaching English as a second or foreign language (ESL/EFL), or teaching another second or foreign language (e.g. Chinese or Spanish) is that there are few opportunities for career advancement. As a consequence, many language teachers spend a lot of their time just trying to get better at the same job over their careers. Indeed, many of the contexts you may find yourself teaching in over the years (e.g. K–12 schools, universities, language schools, or institutions that offer weekend courses in language learning and teaching) do not really encourage teachers to ask questions about their careers; many times the administrators just want teachers to keep the students or clients happy so that the department or school/institution can continue to receive good reviews or to make as much money as possible. I realize that not all language departments, schools, or institutions are like this; but for many in language teaching, and especially in the ESL/EFL field, learning and teaching language is a big business throughout the world and the focus is not on standards. In some countries, advertisements for "native speaker English language teachers" have as a qualification that the teacher be young; and if they are attractive, this is a bonus. Terms such as "backpacker teachers" have arisen over the years in the English teaching industry because people who run some profit-making schools only want their teachers to be able to speak English (even if their vocabulary and grammar are suspect) and also to "look like" an English

Reflection Journal 1.3

First, write your own answers to these questions, and then find a partner or a group to discuss your findings and reflections; after these discussions in a pair or group, write a paragraph about your concluding reflections.

- What does or should a language teacher look like?
- What are the most important things a teacher needs to know to be able to teach a second or foreign language (in general or a specific one)?
- Where can a teacher get information about these things?
- Do you think you know everything you need to know about language teaching now that you have been teaching for some time?
- Or do you think you know (or will know) all you need to because you are (or soon will be) newly qualified as a teacher and have the knowledge gained from all your courses to get you through the rest of your career as a teacher?
- I was told once by an EFL teacher in Asia that he did not know what all the fuss was about techniques and methodology and professional development in language teaching; he said that all you had to do was talk to the students in English and they would pick it up. How would you respond to this comment?

teacher (whatever that means!). Given the lack of standards in some parts of the English teaching industry throughout the world, teachers may think again, why bother with professional development? Does anyone care about the students?

Some teachers may try to respond to the notion of teacher development, which they may see as this "annoying idea of developing as a teacher," with the suggestion that they already know it all because they have been teaching for a long time. (Or is it really just that they have been successful keeping the students happy, or quiet?) Let us look at this latter reasoning for a moment. Let's say that you have been teaching now for some time and you have had so many different experiences with your work both inside and outside the classroom that you feel you are now able to go on "autopilot" (i.e. follow routine without thinking) while you are teaching a class. You have done this so often in your classrooms in the past few years that you now begin to think to yourself that the students you teach are really all the same, and all you need to do is to plug in the techniques you have used so many times in the past and sit back and watch; it usually works. You may also get to the point that you begin to think your second or foreign language students all make the same language mistakes, and so you just prepare your classes the same way, by using the same techniques and methods, because you are, after all, on autopilot – even though you may have been given a different textbook for the different classes you teach.

Indeed, you may have come to the point now in your teaching career when you wake up in the morning before class and realize (should you pause for any reflection) that you may be numb both to and in your teacher role. Or as one teacher reflected to me, he just realized that he was teaching what he called "mind-numbing conversation classes." Even this realization is a beginning step to teacher reflection, as the teacher is aware that something is wrong in his classes. He is now wondering why he became a teacher in the first place and even why he was initially excited to meet all of the different students who have now blended into one mass that he thinks he knows and can predict how they will all perform in his class. This is in fact a true story, but with a positive outcome: the teacher changed completely after this realization. The same can be true for many more teachers if they try to wake up to what is really happening in their classrooms.

Reflection Journal 1.4

First, write your own answers to these questions, and then find a partner or a group to discuss your findings and reflections; after these discussions in a pair or group, write a paragraph about your concluding reflections.

- Do you feel a need to take more control of your professional life?
- If you answer yes to the above question, what made you think or realize this? Did a particular critical incident happen or some other event that made you reflect on your professional life?
- Do you know how you can take more control of your professional life as a teacher?
- Do you think that reflecting on your teaching (both inside and outside the classroom) can help you take more control of your professional life? If so, how?

Waking Up

Teachers may begin to realize that they need to change something in their professional lives at some stage of their professional careers, but they may not be sure what that change is or if in fact they really want to bother. This sense of unease may last a short time or a long time before individual teachers begin to seriously consider where they are professionally. I had this same feeling of unease after about five years of teaching experience as I realized that I was following routine in how I set up my ESL classes, regardless of the class I was teaching: I figured I knew my students well before they had even entered my classroom, I had all my usual techniques for group work and pair work ready for use, and I had the same jokes ready to get an easy laugh. But then it all changed one day when I was teaching as usual and something really hit me (a critical incident of sorts): the students were all responding as I had anticipated, or at least how I thought they should, and I realized when I was using groups that I *really did not know* what my students were learning in terms of language development. Yes, they were *acting* the way I wanted them to act, but were they practicing English or just practicing their mistakes? Were they really developing their English or were they actually stuck in some stage of language acquisition? I was not sure because over the previous five years, I had become so engrossed in teaching methods and control of classes (of course, I did not realize this!) that I had never really reflected on the substance or linguistic results of my teaching.

At this point of sudden realization (I think I still remember the actual class this occurred in), I became very uneasy about my whole approach to my work – to the point that I became apprehensive about my own methodology. I realized that I did not really know what I was doing or what my students were learning, and worse, I did not know how to go about looking into all this. Although I was putting into practice what I had learned in graduate school, I realized then that I had never really reflected on my teaching or the results of my teaching in terms of my students' learning. When I was a student teacher, I had just assumed that the techniques and methods we were learning in education courses would automatically work in any setting. Why wouldn't they, as these teacher educators were the experts, and they would not have taught these techniques and methods to us if they were not useful, or so I thought! I remember I was upset that my professional world was now disturbed, as I thought I had my teaching all figured out up to then and all I had to do was coast, do what I always did in my classes and enjoy my students and life in general. From time to time, someone would join our faculty with new qualifications and bring in journals such as *ELT Journal* or *TESOL Quarterly*, but I did not want to (or need to) read these journals about new methods and practices and theories from this field called TESOL or Applied Linguistics. I had my routine down and it worked for me, so what would I gain by reading articles? Anyway, I was already a qualified teacher. Yet that uneasy feeling stayed with me and was always there bothering me, so eventually I decided to do something about it. Before I continue with my story about what happened next in my own professional development, now is a good time for you to begin your own reflections about your career as a language teacher.

Reflection Journal 1.5

First, write your own answers to these questions, and then find a partner or a group to discuss your findings and reflections; after these discussions in a pair or group, write a paragraph about your concluding reflections.

- How long have you been a language teacher?
- What initial teacher education have you had and when?
- What other professional development different from an initial qualification do you have as a teacher?
- Do you ever spend much time thinking about your teaching?

Are most teachers self-motivated to actually think about what they do as teachers, or are they the opposite, demotivated in their work? Individual teachers can give many reasons for lack of motivation in their work: incompetent or unkind and difficult administrators, low pay, too many contact hours, a lack of support from the institution or university; or some will say they are just teaching for the money – this is a job and not a profession. I too had experienced negativity from administrators whose sole reason for running language schools was to make money and whose philosophy for teachers was that they would be tolerated as long as they could keep the students (read: fee-paying clients) happy. I have met some EFL teachers, backpackers really, who were only too eager to keep the students happy so that they could make some money regardless of what they were doing, or not doing, in their classrooms. I have also met some great teachers in my time who really cared about their students and their teaching and the whole idea of what they were doing in their classrooms. An academic advisor of mine once pointed out that there are three types of teachers: (a) those who stay in teaching for a while and then get bored and quit; (b) those who are bored and complain about their lot but keep doing the same old thing without any reflection or change – some may even have an illusion of happiness that all is going well; or (c) those who realize that they can become genuine *educators* by reflecting on their actions, changing what they do in response to circumstances, and growing towards true inner peace. The latter teachers, the educators, are truly professional and are doing the best job possible, accepting that they will never know it all. This chapter (and this book) is directed at and dedicated to the third type of teacher who is interested in his or her own professional development. To reach level c, teachers must wake up to what they are doing in their classrooms.

I am the first to admit that it is not easy to *wake up* to new ways of thinking and reflecting, new ideas about how to teach and opening ourselves to new theories of teaching and learning. One person told me a story about the difficulty of waking up that captures the situation: imagine that it is 3:00 am and someone is trying to rouse you from your sleep because they want to tell you something important (Maybe the house is in fire!). You are in the middle of a wonderful dream, all is well, and you feel great so you are hoping this person will just go away and leave you alone, regardless of what is going on that they need to wake you up about. That half-sleep of wanting reality to go away is exactly what waking up to teacher development and reflective practice seeks to address – you don't want to know; you just want it to go away because you are comfortable now in following routine. Yes, I too felt like I wanted the wake-up to stop so I could go back to my own sweet dreams. But when you as a teacher do wake up and realize what exactly is going on, and has been going on for some time, in your own classes and how you can rise even higher as a result of waking up and achieving a level of new awareness, then you will know, once you have achieved a new reflective state, that it has been worth it.

Reflection Journal 1.6

First, write your own answers to these questions, and then find a partner or a group to discuss your findings and reflections; after these discussions in a pair or group, write a paragraph about your concluding reflections.

- Do you ever feel as if you need to wake up from your teaching dreams?
- Do you want to wake up?
- Do you ever feel helpless about your teaching situation and your role as a language teacher? If so, why?

Noticing: The Starting Point of Professional Development

When I looked around me as a young teacher and began to realize that not everyone was in the language teaching profession (yes, I think language teaching is a profession) for the purposes of helping students learn, I still had an uneasy feeling that I had no idea what was happening in my classes and was a bit anxious about what to do. I knew that I had to do something, such as examine what I was doing in some way, or go into a different profession. So I promised myself to give language teaching another year to see what would happen, as I began to examine all aspects of my work in detail. I decided to take the plunge and begin looking at my own teaching and taking notice of what was happening in my classes, but I had no idea how to go about it. I decided to write a journal regularly about what I was thinking about my work in general and what I noticed in my classes, and then to see what would emerge from these journal entries after a month or so. Of course, I did not tell anyone I was doing this since it could seem as if I was not a good teacher because I was questioning what I was doing.

After I had looked for about a month at my own everyday teaching activities that I routinely carried out based on my five years of teaching experience, I noticed that I was slowly becoming more attuned to many other aspects of my work which I was totally unaware of previously such as the different types, functions, and effects of my questions; the number of each different type of question that I routinely asked; the impact on student participation of different classroom seating organization structures in the room; my correction techniques; my types of teacher talk; and many more such features of my teaching that occurred every day, seemingly habitually in my classes. As I began to look more at my own practice during the course of my regular teaching activities, I started to realize that I was becoming more attuned to what was going on: I began to engage in the discipline of noticing (Mason, 2002). I began to learn from noticing events in my own work rather than being brought along by others, and I began to think about new approaches to my practice. I started to get the courage to talk to other teachers about what I had noticed because I was curious about whether they had noticed similar features of their

Reflection Journal 1.7

First, write your own answers to these questions, and then find a partner or a group to discuss your findings and reflections; after these discussions in a pair or group, write a paragraph about your concluding reflections.

- What is your reaction to the term, *professional development*?
- Have you ever engaged in any form of professional development?
- If your answer is yes to the previous question, explain it; if your answer is no, why have you not considered any form of professional development up to now in your career?
- How would you advise a language teacher to engage in professional development?

own teaching and what their results were, and I wondered what we could do about improving our teaching. I had in fact, and without knowing or realizing it at the time, entered into my own period of professional development.

When I mention professional development to some teachers, they seem to retreat physically a bit (and I imagine mentally, too) from me, as if it is a medication they had to take to remedy some problem they have. In many countries, professional development is a requirement for most teachers at some time in their careers, so that they can meet their licensing requirements and/or because it is a school requirement for an in-service day (sometimes called a Professional Development or PD day) when teachers have no teaching responsibilities but must come to school to learn about new educational ideas; the PD day often consists of presentation of ideas in the form of workshops delivered by an outside "expert." This I term *top-down* professional development because it is mandated from above, by the school administration. The main idea of these school-mandated workshops is that the knowledge and new ideas teachers receive from so-called outside experts could (or even should) later be regurgitated because this knowledge is said to be the current "truth." What happens in most cases, however, is that the teachers reject these ideas because they have little or no meaning for specific classrooms or teaching situations. In this type of top-down approach to professional development, teachers can also meet their license requirements by taking courses at a local college or university; participating in district-organized training programs; and/or attending seminars, conferences, and workshops outside the school. What I have observed many times during these courses and workshops is that teachers take a more social view of their development by renewing acquaintance with their peers and talking shop (usually in the form of comparing pay and benefits, rather than teaching methods) with other teachers over coffee or lunch. This is all good; however, when asked later what they have learned at any of the above-mentioned events that they have since used in their classrooms in some way and that resulted in meaningful change in their practice, not many say that they have used anything they learned in any meaningful way beyond some "quick-fix" scenarios. As Fullan (1991: 315) has noted: "Nothing has promised so much and has been so frustratingly wasteful as the thousands of workshops and conferences that led to no significant change in practice when the teachers returned to their classrooms."

Professional Development: *Top-Down or Bottom-Up?*

The term *professional development* has been used so often within the field of Education that it has lost some of its potential, not to mention, its meaning because there is not an agreed upon definition (I will outline what I think is a good definition later in this section) that is also concrete and applicable to practice. Although it is thirty years or so since it was first mentioned, this term remains, according to Evans (2002: 123), "ill-defined." Educators have seen as a result of this lack of conceptual clarity an explosion of different approaches to professional development that have not always provided administrators and teachers with improvements in teaching. Indeed, an early legacy of confusion in the literature as to what exactly professional development involves has resulted in somewhat of a division of approach regarding who should initiate professional development programs – school administrators or the teachers themselves. The first approach, which I've referred to as a *top-down approach*, is usually initiated by school administrators or people who are responsible for developing curriculum, such as Ministry or Department of Education officials in different countries or states. Such an approach usually involves a process in which teachers are informed by others (generally outside experts and/or university professors) about changes and developments in the knowledge base of their profession and then told that these changes should be transferred and fully incorporated into their future instructional practices. The second approach to professional development is a *bottom-up approach* in which teachers initiate the process to inform themselves by investigating their practices and beliefs so that they can construct their own theories of teaching and learning. Because this division of top-down vs. bottom-up within the professional development literature has important philosophical implications for both administrators and teachers alike, I will continue the discussion on the differences between the traditional top-down approach and the non-traditional bottom-up approach and briefly outline what has been discussed in the literature about both. Then I will outline how we can in fact use both approaches for professional development by including an example from my own work in second language teaching. I will be emphasizing the bottom-up approach to reflective practice throughout the remainder of this book. The main point I am trying to make here is that both approaches can be used together to help language teachers achieve their main goal of providing effective learning opportunities for their students in their classrooms.

Reflection Journal 1.8

First, write your own answers to these questions, and then find a partner or a group to discuss your findings and reflections; after these discussions in a pair or group, write a paragraph about your concluding reflections.

- Top-down professional development has often consisted of teachers taking graduate courses, attending outside conferences or workshops, or engaging in several Professional Development (PD) days set aside in the school calendar for these events. List some of the courses, conferences, workshops, and school PD events you have attended.
- What impact did each of these have on your immediate teaching?
- Which had the most impact and which had the least impact, and why?
- Can you think of any other top-down professional development events you attended and the impact they could have had but did not have on your teaching, and why?

Top-Down Approach

In its traditional form, professional development for many teachers has often involved further graduate work, attending conferences, seminars, workshops, and special professional development days (PD Days) that many schools build into the calendar. Attendance at these activities is then recorded in the teacher's personnel file and checks are placed beside the teacher's professional development requirement/quota with the (mis)understanding by administrators that the teacher has learned new skills and has therefore changed his or her teaching as a result. Yet more often than not, there is no real change in the teacher (although there may be observable small changes in teaching behaviors) because the individual teacher is not really involved in the professional development process. This is because there is no significant personal investment by individual teachers when attending these seminars, workshops, and even the in-house PD days, as they have been mandated by others.

The top-down approach to professional development is considered goal-oriented in that experts are called in to a school or school district to give talks and workshops on curricular changes or new teaching methods and to demonstrate how particular instructional practices should be implemented. This approach to teacher development is sometimes referred to as a *deficit model* of professional development because the teachers are considered to have some deficit (defined by administrators and outside experts rather than the teachers themselves) in how they are teaching, with the understanding that this can be "fixed" by having them attend these workshops. In reality, what usually transpires is that most teachers find the so-called "deficit" topics and related workshop activities to be of little or no relevance for their particular classrooms, but they must attend these workshops in order to fulfill their PD obligations or simply because they have been told to attend. These top-down approaches to professional development generally have only superficial results because meaningful, long-term changes involve initiatives by the participants themselves. When teachers are presented with new teaching ideas at mandated workshops, what usually happens is that they reject them outright or attempt to regurgitate them without any reflection as to their impact on student learning and without taking any professional responsibility for making sure the transfer of these new ideas to their classrooms is successful. Unfortunately, this type of implementation is likely to fail, and the teacher is likely to become even more disillusioned with the whole idea of professional development. Some of this disillusionment probably arises from the idea that the top-down imposed professional development is designed by the administrators to be "teacher-proof," so that they (the administrators) can control how the teachers develop.

Reflection Journal 1.9

First, write your own answers to these questions, and then find a partner or a group to discuss your findings and reflections; after these discussions in a pair or group, write a paragraph about your concluding reflections.

- What is your experience of attending courses and/or workshops that have been mandated by administrators or others?
- What benefits did you receive and what did you learn from these?
- Did you implement any of the activities you were presented at the workshops? Explain why or why not. Describe how you implemented these activities and how long they lasted.
- All teachers are faced with so many changes in various aspects of their work, from the moment they graduate from their course of study, that they were not, and could not, be prepared for in advance. What changes have you noticed in your teaching situation since you have graduated?
- Can you outline some of the changes that have taken place in technology, theory, or practice of second language or reading, or in theory of sociolinguistics or second language acquisition that have implications for teaching?

Bottom-Up Approach

The top-down approach to professional development can be seen as an attempt by some administrators, and indeed textbook publishers as well, to control teachers by imposing teaching approaches and set curriculum that is "teacher-proof" and as a way to "fix" teachers or fill in their information gaps. Sometimes we hear the terms *teacher training* and *teacher development* in discussions about professional development, and many times they are taken to mean the same thing; however, they are not the same thing because, as Richards and Farrell (2005) have suggested, training is more short-term, and is usually delivered by outside experts and is thus considered a top-down form of professional development. A *training approach* to professional development assumes that supervisors and workshop leaders know what good teaching is

Reflection Journal 1.10

First, write your own answers to these questions, and then find a partner or a group to discuss your findings and reflections; after these discussions in a pair or group, write a paragraph about your concluding reflections.

- What is your understanding of the terms *teacher training* and *teacher development*?
- What is your understanding of *bottom-up professional development*?
- Have you ever experienced this type of professional development? If yes, explain. If no, how do you think you would go about this?
- Read the example below of *Communicating with colleagues of a different culture* and consider the situation I faced as a director of these part-time teachers.

Communicating with Colleagues of a Different Culture

I was teaching in a small university in Seoul, Korea, some years ago and found myself in charge of 25 part-time Korean ESL teachers. I soon realized that I was *communicating with colleagues of a different culture*. Because I was the first non-Korean director of the program, the instructors did not know what to expect, and neither did I know what to expect or to do in this new context. I had learned that previous teacher meetings with a Korean director of the program consisted of giving the instructors their syllabi and telling them to teach on this basis; and the instructors had not had any meetings during the semester or during the year to discuss their classes. What had developed over the years was the formation of different subgroups of teachers (usually arranged by age) who informally discussed things about their work at lunch or in the teachers' room, but there was no interaction or discussion between these groups. Immediately, I tried to establish better collaboration by having more teacher meetings on topics, usually topics I had thought important. Because everybody came to these meetings, at first I was pleased. However, it soon became apparent that I was doing all of the talking at the meetings, even when the teachers broke up into small groups. When I tried to institute a system of peer observation, I was indirectly told, "This is not the Korean way," or "It will not work." And indeed it did not. To solve this dilemma, I tried a few different methods, some of which succeeded and others that were only marginally successful. For example, I tried to meet the teachers "by chance," outside my office to see who would be interested to talk about teaching and who might be interested in sharing their views about the program. What follows is a summary of what developed over the course of the following weeks.

and that participating teachers will have to change their teaching behaviors to meet their expectations. *Training* thus contrasts with *development*, which refers to the acquisition of awareness and attitudes by individual language teachers and thus has more of a personal perspective. Teachers have their own concerns and issues related to their classrooms, and these they feel should be addressed in any professional development program. Development is an

About teaching: Teachers were encouraged to bring any lesson plans that had been successful for them in the past and to place them in a file for others to use if they wanted. I also put my lesson plans in the file as examples for anyone to follow. Some teachers placed some lesson plans in the file, but not many, as this was not the culture of teachers in that school, So the cabinet remained nearly empty, and the idea fizzled out eventually. But in the process, I did manage to generate some informal discussions about teaching and the idea of talking about teaching and learning in the program, as some of the teachers shared some ideas about their teaching and the program. Related to the program, I learned, for example, that the teachers were very concerned about examinations and how they were designed and administered in the past.

About the program: I started an exam committee among interested teachers in the school so that we could all share in the examination process in the program. Most of the teachers seemed very interested in this initiative and many volunteered to serve on the committee. From this point on, the exam committee, with input from the other teachers, decided on the design and implementation of all future English examinations in the school. This worked because teachers had a vested interest, in that their students were going to take these exams.

Serendipity: From the committee mentioned above, I also discovered that a smaller group of teachers were interested not only in the program and exams, but also in their own teacher development; so after some coaxing by me, they decided to start a teacher development group. These five teachers met with me (as group facilitator) regularly over the remainder of the semester to discuss their practice in more detail.

- Why do you think the teachers did not become involved in adding lesson plans to the file for others to see and possibly use?
- Why do you think they wanted to become involved in the exam committee?
- Why did it take a long time for the five teachers to form a teacher development group to share their ideas about teaching?
- Is this an example of a bottom-up or top-down teacher approach to teacher development? Explain your answer.

evolving process of learning, growth, and change and is based on a teacher's personal experiences and reflections of teaching. As such, it is considered a bottom-up approach to professional development (Farrell, 2007). Professional development programs that are initiated by the teachers themselves can empower teachers to implement changes that they think are necessary because these changes are based on systematic reflections of their own practices in their own classrooms. Thus, a bottom-up approach to professional development is voluntary and is based on systematic reflections on practice that can foster voluntary teacher change which is sustained throughout a teacher's career.

The above example in the set of reflective questions raises the issue of which is the most effective approach to professional development for teachers, top-down or bottom-up? In a commentary on the particular example above, Professor Richard Day of the University of Hawaii had this to say:

> I agree that top down approaches generally have only superficial results and that meaningful, long term changes involve initiatives by the participants. But it turns out that in this case both approaches seem to have worked. The exam committee was the result of top down action: the program head, Farrell, set up the committee; it was on his initiative that it was established. The small discussion group was the result of a bottom up process: some of the teachers …began talking with one another about their teaching.
>
> (Farrell, 1998: 128)

So it seems then that both top-down and bottom-up approaches were in play in the case above.

Sustaining Professional Development

Guskey's (2000: 16) definition of teacher professional development as the "process and activities designed to enhance the professional knowledge, skills, and attitude of educators so that they might, in turn, improve the learning of students" seems closest to the emphasis and framework of the material presented in this book because it focuses on improving student learning (rather than teaching in the abstract). If we look at teacher development from the perspective of student learning, then it may be easier to sustain throughout a teacher's career because students are never the same in any one class, on any one day, or in any one teaching term or year. Professional development is a process that never ends because teachers never cease learning about their students, about themselves as teachers, and about new developments in their field. As Underhill (1999: 17) suggests, professional development is "the process of becoming the best teacher one is able to be; a process that can be started but never finished." As people begin their teaching careers, they may not see this and may rather think that they have "arrived" at being a teacher. Novice teachers who have just gone through their initial education often start their first teaching job with thoughts that they have been armed with all of the latest methods and techniques and are thus knowledgeable to be able to teach forever. Teachers who have been teaching for many years, in contrast, realize that they never really know it all and must stand back at different times in their careers to reflect on where they are. Thus, you as a teacher can enter into periods of intensive self-reflection during your career to observe where you are at a particular point in time, whether the result is where you want to be, and where you want to go from that point onwards.

Reflection Journal 1.11

First, write your own answers to these questions, and then find a partner or a group to discuss your findings and reflections; after these discussions in a pair or group, write a paragraph about your concluding reflections.

- When you graduated with your teaching or other graduate qualification, did you think you knew it all and that you had enough information to sustain you throughout your career?
- Are you the kind of teacher you want to be at this stage of your career?
- If your answer is yes, how do you know (what is the evidence you see for this)?
- If your answer is no, why do you say this?
- What sort of changes (if any) do you think you need to incorporate into your practice, and why?
- Where do you see yourself as a language teacher in three to five years time?
- How will you get there?

In order for professional development programs to be truly successful, they must also have value to each individual teacher, and as such must be *self-reflective* if they are to be supported by these teachers and sustained over a longer period of time. As Head and Taylor (1997: 1; emphasis in original) have noted, development is "*a self-reflective* process, because it is through questioning old habits that alternative ways of being and doing are able to emerge." Teachers who want to implement a bottom-up approach to professional development usually also want to direct their own learning and development independently and to do so on an individual basis. Sometimes this self-reflection begins with an idea that they want to learn more about a particular teaching strategy which they may have read about or have seen in some workshop or other PD event. In other words, they *notice* something in their practice that gets their attention and they want to, or feel the need to, do something about it.

One of the simplest ways individual teachers can begin a process of self-reflection is to engage in writing about whatever dilemmas they may be facing on the job. However, you do not have to focus on dilemmas; you can also focus on successes or what has worked for you, so that you reflect on all aspects of your work equally and with the same emotion. The act of writing can also be very cathartic as it begins a process of unburdening your thoughts so that you can actually *see* what it is you may be thinking. This can be liberating for many because what you think you see and what you actually see many not be the same. So writing allows some distance from your thoughts. Of course, you can also videotape and audiotape your classes and thus also see (in a different light) what may be happening in your classes; and you can write about this, too, and your reflections on what you see. You will be doing a lot of self-reflective writing as you continue to read the contents of this book with the use of such reflective tools as a teaching journal, constructing a teaching portfolio, and engaging in action research as you enter into intensive exploration, examination, and reflection on your practice.

Richards and Farrell (2005) speak of a *teaching journal* as a notebook in which a teacher writes regularly about teaching experiences and other events. I maintain that journal writing can help language teachers question and analyze what they do both inside and outside the classroom because it is the very process of writing that helps teachers to consciously explore and analyze their practice. McDonough (1994: 64–65) maintains that teachers who write regularly about their teaching can become more aware of "day-to-day behaviors and underlying attitudes, alongside outcomes and the decisions that all teachers need to take."

Action research, which comes under the umbrella of reflective practice, is the focused investigation of a particular aspect of teaching that may be causing some problem in a particular teacher's classes. It is all about doing research and taking action to improve teaching. The process of action research involves a teacher entering a cycle of research that is focused on solving a perceived problem until the teacher reaches a certain level of reflective awareness about that problem to enable him or her make changes that improve practice. Wallace (1991: 56–57) maintains that action research can have a "specific and immediate outcome which can be directly related to practice in the teacher's own context" and is "an extension of the normal reflective practice of many teachers, but it is slightly more rigorous and might conceivably lead to more effective outcomes." As a result of entering into a cycle of action research, a teacher has enough information about a specific problem to be able to make informed decisions about what he or she will do in future classes, and the teacher will continue to monitor these decisions until it no longer is a problem for the teacher or his or her students.

As mentioned above, reflection can be done alone (solo) but can also be done with others collaboratively, either with another teacher such as in a *critical friendship* or with three or more teachers in a group. There are advantages and disadvantages to reflecting solo or with others; the main advantage to reflecting with others is that what individual teachers think they see and what they actually see may not be the same thing, and when reflecting with others, teachers can be challenged when this occurs. Head and Taylor (1997: 91) define a *teacher development group* as "any form of co-operative and ongoing arrangement between two or more teachers to work together on their own personal and professional development." When language teachers come together in a group of two or more collaborators, they can help each other to articulate their thoughts about their work so that they can all grow professionally together (Farrell, 2007). Research has indicated that language teacher development groups facilitate dialogue, sharing, and collaboration, as well as the exchange of resources, information, and expertise.

Stages in Sustaining Professional Development

Some teachers may not want to reflect with other teachers, especially when they start reflecting on their work, because of fear of revealing themselves to others. This is a very real fear for many people and as such should be addressed by all teachers before they enter into reflections with others. I will not be insisting on collaboration in this book because I think it is up to each teacher to decide when and if he or she is ready to collaborate with other teachers regarding professional development. For example, teachers may want to start by developing on their own; and when and if comfortable with self-reflection, teachers can consider reflecting with their students, with colleagues, with their administrator(s), with teacher organizations, or with others (e.g. online teacher groups). Teachers can follow five stages or cycles of reflection, described below, that can help sustain their professional development.

Stage I

Usually teachers begin their self-reflections by examining their beliefs, values, and assumptions for teaching and by looking at their goals for personal and professional development. Teachers can write about these and then examine their classroom practices in light of their initial self-reflections and make any adjustments to their practices if they are seen to be in conflict with their beliefs and values; or, if they think their practices are effective, they can consider restating their beliefs so that they match these practices. All of these self-reflections can be compiled in a teaching portfolio, so that individual teachers have an ongoing record of their reflections, which they can update as they develop during their teaching careers. In sum, self-reflection means taking stock of who you are as a language teacher, who you have become, and if you like what you find when you carefully examine all your beliefs, values, and classroom practices.

Stage II

The second stage of professional development sees teachers expanding their self-reflections to include reflecting with their students. This is accomplished by paying special attention to all of your students and observing how they learn, how they interact with each other, and what they think about you as a teacher. Each of your students has preferred learning styles and strategies, and it is in your best interest as a teacher to get to know what they like and do not like if you want your lessons to be effective. Indeed, it would be a good idea to ask your students to tell you their preferred roles for you as a language teacher; you may be surprised what they think about what you should be doing in class rather than what you think is good for them.

Stage III

The third stage in professional development sees teachers reflecting with students and their colleagues. Teachers begin to talk to their colleagues about their teaching and to ask them what they are doing in their classes. During this step, you can also consider entering into peer observations, coaching/mentoring, or team teaching situations with colleagues in order to further your own knowledge of your practice. You can even consider setting up teacher development groups with your colleagues within your school or with like-minded colleagues in other regions in order to reflect on your practice. The idea here is that this step promotes collegiality and collaboration in what is often considered a solitary profession: one teacher and twenty or so students in a room behind closed doors. When you include your colleagues, you can have more exchange of resources, more collaboration, and more development of expertise within your school.

Stage IV

The fourth stage, often omitted in second language education, seeks to include the school/institution administration in the teachers' total reflections. Teachers readily include the administration when complaining about teaching conditions and pay, but they rarely include them when they talk about their teaching. Yet, if you think about it, the administration is a very important part of your reflection plan, especially if you want to get acknowledgement for any suggested changes you may consider necessary as a result of your self-reflections or collaborative reflections. For example, if you want to change a textbook for a particular class, you may have to get approval from the administration because they are the ones who generally prescribe the books. So it is better to include the administration in your reflective circle from the very beginning so that they can see how professional you teachers in their school really are.

Stage V

The fifth stage sees teachers reflecting with and within their profession and professional organizations, which for an EFL or ESL teacher would mean the big two: TESOL, Teachers of English to Speakers of Other Languages, based in the United States, and/or IATEFL, the International Association of Teachers of English as a Foreign Language, based in the United Kingdom. For foreign language (FL) teachers, the primary organization is the Modern Language Association (MLA), but there are also specialized organizations for the different languages taught. There are also many country, regional, and local professional organizations as well that you can become involved with for your professional development. You should include the most relevant professional organization(s) in your reflections as you attempt to link your results to what others have found in different contexts. In this way, language education policy can develop from all sectors of the globe and not just from the ideas and

Reflection Journal 1.12

First, write your own answers to these questions, and then find a partner or a group to discuss your findings and reflections; after these discussions in a pair or group, write a paragraph about your concluding reflections.

- Have you ever developed any individualized professional development plan over the years?
- Which of the stages discussed above do you think you would like to try in order to reflect on your practice, and why?
- Go through each stage above and list how you can reflect within each stage and who or what organization you can reflect with (after stage I).
- Have you read anything recently related to your work that has made you interested in exploring further, such as a new teaching strategy or assessment tool?
- If yes, how would you go about reflecting on this within each of the five stages outlined above?
- Have you ever written a journal on issues related to your work?
- Do you like writing in general?
- Do you think the act of writing can be cathartic?
- Have you ever videotaped or audiotaped your classes?
- Have you ever engaged in an action research topic?
- Have you ever worked collaboratively with other teachers on your professional development?
- List some of the advantages and disadvantages of working solo and collaboratively on your professional development.
- How can you overcome some of the disadvantages you have listed above?
- Have you ever gone to a professional conference? If yes, what were your impressions of the conference? If not, why not?
- Have you ever presented at a professional conference? If yes, explain. If not, would you like to present? (After you read this book, I am hoping you will have more than one topic to share with other teachers at professional conferences.)

practices of some dominant professionals in particular countries. When you have entered into one of the preceding cycles of reflection, you now have the opportunity at this stage of writing the results and your reflections of the process and presenting these at one of your professional organization conferences. This can show that you have something to contribute to your field, and I expect other teachers will be eager to hear from you.

You can also try to publish your reflections in a professional journal or edited volume from one of your professional organizations. An example of this is when I started the Language Teacher Research (LTR) series within the TESOL organization in which I attempted to encourage practicing teachers from all parts of the globe to reflect on their work and then to report their reflections by following a template that mapped out subheadings they would follow when reporting their findings and reflections. We ended up with six volumes of LTR that stretched from the Americas, to Asia, Australia/New Zealand, Africa, Europe, and the Middle East. I am very pleased that we were able to accomplish this because it is the first attempt from any of our professional organizations to try to include so many diverse contexts within one series, and it celebrates the achievements of the many teachers working at all different levels within each context. I will return to this series, which is part of my own professional development in the way of publishing and also outreach to other teachers, in the final chapter of this book.

Conclusion

Teacher professional development as defined in this chapter and book is much more than attending conferences, one-stop workshops, and seminars (although it can include these, too). Rather, it involves teachers looking intensively and systematically at their practice, and as such it involves a personal investment by each teacher into defining what the term *professional development* means for him or her (bottom-up approach). This type of bottom-up professional learning and development is seen as “mental growth spurred from within” (Feiman-Nemser and Floden, 1986: 523), as teachers are supported in their own directions of growth in the form of self-directed learning and development. Such support in reality involves both a top-down approach and a bottom-up approach to teacher development: the top-down feature is for continued support from institutions and administrators to allow individual (or groups of) teachers to pursue their own (bottom-up) investigations about their practice. Language teachers can engage in this type of development by first looking at themselves as teachers and what they are doing in their classrooms and then considering this information in light of their beliefs. This process of *looking at* and then *reflecting on* can be achieved by an initial *top-down push*; however, the only real, that is, meaningful and lasting, professional

Chapter 1 Reflections

First, write your own answers to these questions, and then find a partner or a group to discuss your findings and reflections; after these discussions in a pair or group, write a paragraph about your concluding reflections after reading this chapter.

- Do you think you or other teachers change their practices after going through a certificate or Masters degree course? If yes, how do you think these courses influence teaching? If not, why not?
- Smith, Hofer, Gillespie, Solomon, and Rowe (2003: 36) have suggested in the conclusion of their *How Teachers Change* study, "This study demonstrates that professional development, while necessary, is not sufficient by itself to drive changes in practice. Professional development is one tool for change but needs to be offered within a context that supports teachers to make change." Why do you think teachers may find it difficult to change their teaching practices even after engaging in different forms of professional development? What kind(s) of support do you think teachers would need to make changes in their teaching practices?
- Freeman (1993) explored how four high school teachers of French and Spanish responded to the new ideas encountered on their in-service M.A. degree course. Although there was clear evidence of changes in some practices, others remained as part of the teachers' old routines. Why do you think routines have such power with teachers? Why do you think some teachers do not change their teaching practices even though they want to or feel the need to change as a result of taking courses or workshops?
- Clarke and Hollingsworth (2002: 948) identify six perspectives on teacher change; comment on each of these and then consider which one(s) would suit your professional development and change.
  - *Change as training* – change is something that is done to teachers; that is, teachers are "changed."
  - *Change as adaptation* – teachers "change" in response to something; they adapt their practices to changed conditions.
  - *Change as personal development* – teachers "seek to change" in an attempt to improve their performance or develop additional skills or strategies.
  - *Change for local reform* – teachers "change something" for reasons of personal growth.
  - *Change as systematic restructuring* – teachers enact the "change policies" of the system.
  - *Change as growth or learning* – "teachers change inevitably through professional activity"; teachers are themselves learners who work in a learning community.
- What is your understanding of professional development now, and what do you expect to discover as you continue reading this book?
- Write a brief draft of how you will organize your professional development as a language teacher.

development will involve individual teachers reflecting on their classrooms from *their own initiative*, i.e. bottom-up. The remainder of this book looks at professional development through reflective practice and through a combination of the five stages of professional development, with writing as the main mode of reflection.

2. Reflective Practice

Preamble

In 1984, I was teaching a university English language class in Seoul, Korea, and I had set up the class similar to what I had been doing in the previous five years: it revolved around a topic for class discussion, with students divided into groups of four and with each group member responsible for different roles, such as group leader, timekeeper, reporter, and group scribe. This system had worked well for me over the years, and the students seemed to like it. This particular class was a high-elementary proficiency level class in which the students were just beginning to get used to speaking in English to each other; all seemed to enjoy the experience, as the class noise levels were high. The class started as usual with the teacher (me) introducing the topic that was to be discussed and the handouts that would provide more detailed information about the topic. Then the groups of four students were formed by random selection, and the groups started reading the handouts and beginning their discussions. After about five minutes, the noise levels got higher in some groups as they became more animated and as I, the teacher began to circle the class and listen to the conversations in individual groups.

I was pleased at the energy levels in all of the groups, but then it hit me for the first time: I did not know what was *really* happening in each group in terms of English language development. Were they developing their English in any true sense, or were they merely practicing their mistakes? Were they listening to mistakes made by their peers and subconsciously taking these incorrect language patterns into their own "personal language grammars," that is, their *interlanguage*? I was not sure when should I correct these mistakes, or whether I *should* correct these mistakes, and if so, when? Would my correcting their mistakes just confuse them and at the same time stop the flow of conversation and even cause them to be reluctant to speak? If I didn't correct them, some of the students might become angry because some thought that I should be correcting all of their mistakes. Prior to this, what I usually did was to write down some major mistakes the groups made and go over them at the end of the class, but I never really learned if this was effective or not.

At this point in time, I suddenly realized that I was just managing a class rather than teaching English language. I was in effect only providing a forum where students could practice what they knew in terms of English language; I was not really improving their knowledge or performance in many ways. This realization made me begin to question everything about my teaching in all of my classes, how much I was really *teaching* and how much I was only testing students' current levels of English proficiency. What was in fact influencing my classroom decision-making, and why? What were my conceptions of my teaching, and where did these come from? For example, I remember reading about Stephen Krashen's work (e.g. Krashen, 1981, 1982, 1985) and his attempts to explain second language acquisition (SLA) by his *Monitor Model* and the concept of *comprehensible input* and how attractive his theory seemed to me at that time; but I also remember asking myself how these notions influenced my teaching and what impact SLA theory had on my students' learning. After all, I believed that teachers teach because they want their students to learn. So I started my own deep reflections for the first time, after five years of teaching: I knew I had arrived at a crossroads of sorts in my professional world.

Initial Reflections

After that classroom and career critical incident raised my awareness along with some pressing questions about my teaching, I decided to look deeper into my teaching and the field of teaching English as a second language (TESL). To gather more information about my teaching, I decided to write a teaching journal for the first time (although I was skeptical about this, as I had never kept any sort of a journal or diary) about the class I mentioned above and also to write whenever I wanted about my teaching in general. I soon noted some patterns developing in my writing that really surprised me; this was the first real evidence I had about my professional life. I became more interested in my teaching, my students' learning, and the field of TESL. For the latter, I decided to become more active in the local teaching organization of Korea TESOL (before this, I had attended only a few meetings). This involvement led me later to complete a Ph.D. in Rhetoric and Linguistics in the United States, with a dissertation on the topic of reflective practice. At the time I started reflecting, there was no real mention in the literature about the term *reflective practice*. As I learned later, this notion was only starting to make a resurgence with the field of Education in the early 1980s, and it was not until the early 1990s that it began to influence the field of TESL and language teaching more generally. So in retrospect, I guess I was on the cutting edge of reflective practice at the time (the 1990s) in looking at my own conceptions of my teaching and what was influencing me at that time in my classroom practice.

Reflection Journal 2.1

First, write your own answers to these questions, and then find a partner or a group to discuss your findings and reflections; after these discussions in a pair or group, write a paragraph about your concluding reflections.

- Have you ever wondered what your students were learning?
- How do you know that they have learned anything in your class?
- Have you ever questioned your own teaching?
- Did you even have a moment (or moments) in teaching a class when you were not sure what was happening? If so, how did you handle this?
- How would you advise novice teachers about their future professional development? How should they prepare for this?

From the preamble to this chapter, you can see that for me reflective practice means teachers taking on more personal responsibility for their classroom decision-making and, when deciding on specific aspects of their practice which they want (or need) to develop, not looking for teaching methods developed by others (so-called experts or publishers). Instead, they will look into what works best for their students' learning needs, thus ensuring a personal investment in development that is at times missing in many cases from the traditionally top-down mandated professional development programs (as discussed in Chapter 1). A reflective teacher is not one who is always merely complaining about the administration, pay, and working conditions, but someone who is constantly looking for ways to improve learning conditions in the classroom so that students will benefit from his or her teaching. The focus of reflective teaching is student learning, so that a reflective teacher embraces professional development opportunities and is in fact always on the lookout for such opportunities. This is because a reflective teacher wants to take responsibility for instructional actions both inside and outside the classroom that are aimed at creating better learning opportunities for the students. This chapter outlines and explains how language teachers can engage in reflective practice activities as part of their professional development opportunities in order to engage in systematic self-assessment of their current practices. On the basis of the discussion in the previous chapter of the concept of professional development for language teachers, the present chapter outlines the "what" and the "how" of reflective practice, that is, the processes involved in reflective practice.

Reflection Journal 2.2

First, write your own answers to these questions, and then find a partner or a group to discuss your findings and reflections; after these discussions in a pair or group, write a paragraph about your concluding reflections.

- Have you heard of the terms *reflective practice* or *reflective teaching*? If so, where did you hear about these, and from whom?
- What is your understanding of the terms *reflective practice* and/or *reflective teaching*?
- What (if any) are the differences between routine teaching and reflective teaching?
- Do you think teachers should reflect?
- If yes, what do you think teachers should reflect on?
- How do you think teachers should reflect?

The Case For Reflective Practice

Why bother reflecting? After all, teachers do not get much recognition from administrators, school boards, or parents – nor even from most of their students. Teachers prepare and try their best in class, and they try to follow the multitudes of mandates sent to them from the department administration, curriculum developers, school boards, government education officials, and everyone else outside their classrooms. They are paid at the lower end of the socioeconomic groups, especially for those with advanced degrees, and they spend unpaid hours preparing and grading papers; so who has time or energy to reflect on their practice? In fact, we may find many teachers who are close to total burnout from their work, feeling lethargic and not motivated to consider anything beyond their paycheck and holiday plans. Yet it is this very feeling of lethargy that brings everything crashing down in an endless spiral of negative behavior that can be eliminated – yes, eliminated, entirely – when teachers begin to reflect on their practice as part of their professional development. I agree with Lange (1990: 249–250), who sees an intimate relationship between teacher reflection and teacher development:

> The reflective process allows developing teachers latitude to experiment within a framework of growing knowledge and experience. It gives them the opportunity to examine their relations with students, their values, their abilities, and their successes and failures in a realistic context. It begins the developing teacher's path toward becoming an "expert teacher."

Teachers who engage in reflective practice can develop a deeper understanding of their teaching, assess their professional growth, develop informed decision-making skills, and become proactive and confident in their teaching. Professional development through reflective practice can be seen as an opportunity for teachers to enter a process of "mental growth spurred from within" (Feiman-Nemser and Floden, 1986: 523), a process in which teachers can expand their knowledge of their practice and thus seek their own growth. Teachers must also be realistic about reflective practice in terms of who can do it, and when. Reflective practice in reality takes place along a continuum of opportunity, and teachers will vary in the opportunity to reflect, given their context and their own personal psychological makeup. Some contexts may make it impossible for teachers to organize together to reflect on their practices, so that teachers may be able to reflect only on their own individual practices and conceptions of their teaching. As a result, I realize that it may be unreasonable to expect all teachers to engage in reflection at every moment or stage of their teaching day or career. However, certain activities that are outlined in this chapter can benefit teachers in their reflections at various stages of their careers.

Reflection Journal 2.3

First, write your own answers to these questions, and then find a partner or a group to discuss your findings and reflections; after these discussions in a pair or group, write a paragraph about your concluding reflections.

- Is it reasonable and practical for teachers to reflect on their practice?
- How often should teachers reflect? Each class? Daily? Weekly? Monthly? Yearly?
- Reflective practice takes place along a continuum, and teachers vary in the opportunity to reflect.
  - How do teachers vary in the opportunity to reflect?
  - How do teachers vary in their ability to reflect?
  - How do teachers vary in their desire to reflect?

Reflective Disposition

Many years ago, the great American educator, John Dewey, called for teachers to take a reflective stance in their work that entails "active, persistent, and careful consideration of any belief or supposed form of knowledge in light of the grounds that support it and the further consequences to which it leads" (Dewey, 1933: 9). Such a reflective stance sees teachers as active decision makers in their classrooms while all the time thinking about creating learning opportunities for their students. Reflective teachers both create and learn from experience, as Dewey (1938: 25) later said, noting that "all genuine education comes through experience." As he also observed, "every experience lives on in further experience" (Dewey, 1938: 27). Teachers not only create their experiences but can also learn from these experiences as they theorize about their practices, which in turn have meaning for future practices.

Reflectivity, as Dewey (1933) conceptualized it, involves three key attributes: *open-mindedness*, *responsibility*, and *wholeheartedness*. In Dewey's definition, open-mindedness makes a teacher open to alternative views and to more than one side of an issue. Responsibility means that teachers will give careful consideration to the consequences of their actions. Wholeheartedness means that teachers are bold in critically evaluating their practice and making meaningful change, overcoming their fears and uncertainties.

Reflection Journal 2.4

First, write your own answers to these questions, and then find a partner or a group to discuss your findings and reflections; after these discussions in a pair or group, write a paragraph about your concluding reflections.

- What experiences have you created as a teacher?
- How can reflecting on these experiences help you as a teacher?
- Is experience as a teacher enough for effective teaching, or is it necessary to reflect on these experiences as well?
- Consider Dewey's three characteristics and to what degree you possess each of these.
  - Open-minded (desire to listen to more sides than one)
  - Responsible (carefully consider the consequences of actions)
  - Wholehearted (seek every opportunity to learn)
- What levels of these characteristics do you possess as a teacher now (high, medium, or low)?
- Which of these characteristics do you need to develop more as you continue to grow as a teacher?
- Do you think it is possible for teachers to be open-minded, responsible, and wholehearted as defined above?
- Which of these would be most difficult for you to attain, and why?
- Can you think of other desirable characteristics which a reflective practitioner should possess?

Recognizing a Reflective Practitioner

One time after a talk I gave on reflective practice, I was asked an interesting question: How would you recognize a reflective practitioner if you encountered one? This interesting question made me reflect for some time after that, trying to come up with an answer. Would there be physical manifestations of reflectivity – for example, a teacher sitting in a corner of a staff room with index finger under the chin, like the Rodin statue, The Thinker, or a teacher looking into a mirror? These manifestations are possible, but to me a reflective teacher is one who recognizes that teaching experiences are created by the teacher and students and can also be reflected on as a means of learning more about one's teaching self. A reflective teacher will try to articulate his or her theories and beliefs about teaching and learning as guiding principles and will also compare these beliefs and espoused theories with actual classroom practices to make sure there is a convergence rather than a divergence between the two. Reflective teachers will regularly articulate their theories of practice, reflect on what they do in the classroom, and narrow any gap between the two. Reflective teachers will also actively seek out other teachers and educators to hear and see what they are doing and thinking while at the same time continuously developing their plans for their own future teaching actions. It may not be possible to recognize a reflective teacher by any physical attributions, but it will be possible to *recognize* a reflective practitioner by the manner in which he or she carries himself or herself professionally: always curious about his or her practice and always willing to share and hear about what others are doing in their classrooms. From these actions, the reflective teacher will also gain *recognition* from his or her students because they will be able to see these attributes daily in their own classroom, as students know their teacher best.

Reflection Journal 2.5

First, write your own answers to these questions, and then find a partner or a group to discuss your findings and reflections; after these discussions in a pair or group, write a paragraph about your concluding reflections.

- How would you recognize a reflective practitioner if you saw one?
- Are there any special attributes that a reflective practitioner must have?

Defining Reflective Practice

There is a longstanding recognition in the field of language education that teachers must continually reshape their knowledge of teaching and learning (Farrell, 2007). This knowledge is developed initially in teacher education programs, and then becomes part of teachers' education throughout their careers through reflective practice (Tedick, 2005). Reflective practice occurs when teachers consciously take on the role of reflective practitioner and subject their own beliefs about teaching and learning to critical analysis, take full responsibility for their actions in the classroom, and continue to improve their teaching practice (Farrell, 2007).

As I have stated elsewhere, "The use of reflective practice in teacher professional development is based on the belief that teachers can improve their own teaching by consciously and systematically reflecting on their teaching experiences" (Farrell, 2008b: 1). As reflective practitioners, teachers can use the data gathered from these systematic reflections. Teachers can "look back on events, make judgments about them, and alter their teaching behaviors in light of craft, research, and ethical knowledge" (Valli, 1997: 70). This type of self-inquiry can, as Richards (1990: 5) maintains, "help teachers move from a level where they may be guided largely by impulse, intuition, or routine, to a level where their actions are guided by reflection and critical thinking." For the purposes of this chapter, I take the Richards and Farrell (2005: 7) definition of *reflection*, as "the process of critical examination of experiences, a process that can lead to a better understanding of one's practices and routines," to be the closest to the spirit of its originator, John Dewey.

Reflection Journal 2.6

First, write your own answers to these questions, and then find a partner or a group to discuss your findings and reflections; after these discussions in a pair or group, write a paragraph about your concluding reflections.

- Why would teachers need to continually reshape their knowledge of teaching and learning?
- How can teachers critically examine their teaching?
- What is your definition of reflective practice after reading so far?

Forms of Reflective Practice

Even though I have outlined some definitions of reflective practice in the previous section, it has been difficult for scholars to reach consensus on a definition of reflection (Farrell, 2008b: 1), even though most agree that some form of reflection is desirable at all levels of teaching. Indeed, it has been difficult to find a consensus on what type of reflective practices can promote teacher development and improved classroom practices (Farrell, 2007; 2008b: 1). As a consequence of these divisions, two different forms of reflection can be found in the literature, each with its supporters: a weak form that encourages reflection at the descriptive level and a strong form that seeks hard evidence on the results of reflection. In its weaker version, reflective practice is a type of thoughtful practice, in which teachers "informally evaluate various aspects of their professional expertise" (Wallace, 1991: 292). We cannot say that this type of informal reflection actually leads to changes in teaching or even improved teaching because we have no hard evidence of a clear connection of reflective thoughts to classroom actions. Such reflective thoughts may well lead to specific changes in classroom behaviors, and these changes may even be improvements on previous teaching behaviors. On the other hand, these informal reflections can lead to difficulties for teachers and even "unpleasant emotions without suggesting any way forward" (Wallace, 1991: 13) for the teacher to be able to deal with these unpleasant emotions. In fact, reflection without any guidance can lead to feelings of helplessness, when teachers feel isolated in an already isolated profession (one teacher in one classroom, with a group of students, and with the door closed). Individual teachers reflecting informally may seem to be the easiest form of reflective practice; but it can also be the most disastrous, as the teacher may eventually want to leave the profession in order to flee from these unpleasant emotions – emotions that may or may not be realistic.

A second, stronger, form of reflection "involves teachers systematically reflecting on their own teaching and taking responsibility for their actions in the classroom" (Farrell, 2008b: 1–2). In this conception of reflection, teachers should "collect data about their teaching, examine their attitudes, beliefs, assumptions, and teaching practices, and use the information obtained as a basis for critical reflection about teaching" (Richards and Lockhart, 1994: 1). In order for teachers to engage in reflective practice as outlined in the stronger version, they must systematically gather information, "hard data," about their practices so that they can make informed decisions about those practices (Farrell, 2008b: 2). In such a stance toward reflection on practice, teachers make their beliefs and assumptions about their practices evident in their analysis of their teaching" (Farrell, 2008b: 2).

Reflection Journal 2.7

First, write your own answers to these questions, and then find a partner or a group to discuss your findings and reflections; after these discussions in a pair or group, write a paragraph about your concluding reflections.

- Do you think it is possible for teachers just to think about their teaching before, during, and after class as reflective practice?
- Which form of reflection (strong or weak) would you follow?
- Do you think it is reasonable to have teachers collect data about their practice?
- What kind of data would be useful for teachers to collect?
- What would be the most difficult aspect of data collection for you as a teacher?
- Can teachers reflect by just thinking about their classroom practices after class such as on the way home? If yes, how can they be sure these practices actually happened in their classroom?

Reflective Practice Activities

Teachers can choose a number of activities that facilitate reflective practice over the course of their professional careers. Each approach outlined below can be used alone or together with peers, depending on each teacher's level of comfort sharing their ideas, issues, and concerns. Each activity promotes reflection in different ways, and some teachers may find particular activities more appealing than others; so it may be a good idea to try each approach one time before deciding on a focus.

Action Research

Action research comes under the umbrella of reflective practice. It involves investigation of some problem a teacher may be experiencing with a particular class, student, curriculum, or teaching method, and it usually generates some practical knowledge for the teacher that is immediate and directly applicable to practice. Teachers can engage in action research alone, or they can collaborate on one particular project or issue; it all depends on how the results will be used by individual teachers. The main motivation behind action research is change to improve practice by solving a perceived problem. In action research, teachers collect concrete evidence about the problem and its possible solution(s) within a cycle of clearly thought-out procedures.

As Bailey (2001: 490) suggests, action research involves "an approach to collecting and interpreting data which involves a clear, repeated cycle of procedures." I suggest the following cycle that teachers can use for action research projects:

- Identify an issue;
- Review the literature on the issue and ask questions to narrow the focus;
- Choose data to be collected and a method of data collection;
- Collect, analyze, and interpret the data selected;
- Develop, implement, and monitor an action plan. (Farrell, 2007)

Following this action research cycle, the teacher first identifies a general issue in teaching (usually perceived as a problem) and turns it into a working statement. "For example, in a speaking class in which not all students participate regularly, the teacher might formulate the following working statement: *Some of the students in my speaking class never seem to take part in speaking activities*" (Farrell, 2008b: 2). As a next step, the teacher rewrites the working statement in the form of a more specific question: *What kinds of speaking activities involve all of the class in speaking?* The teacher then:

- attempts to reflect on what is happening in the classroom by investigating which speaking activities are being used and the types of interaction and language use they generate;
- chooses a procedure for collecting data, such as through observations, recordings, and transcripts;
- gathers the data and analyzes the information to identify patterns and interpret the findings. (Farrell, 2008b: 2)

To investigate the question above, the teacher might, for example, make an audio or video recording of the class which makes clear that the teacher dominates in discussion and in group problem-solving activities. In order to address this teacher dominance of speaking activities, the teacher might develop an action plan that moves away from teacher-fronted activities to incorporate more types of interaction in which students must speak to each other to complete instructional tasks. The teacher then reviews the effects of the action plan, in order to determine the impact of his or her changed practices on student participation in speaking activities. "Through a process that includes planning, observing, analyzing, acting, and reviewing, language teachers can learn a great deal about the nature of classroom teaching and learning and also acquire useful classroom investigation skills" (Farrell, 2008b: 2).

Reflection Journal 2.8

First, write your own answers to these questions, and then find a partner or a group to discuss your findings and reflections; after these discussions in a pair or group, write a paragraph about your concluding reflections.

- Why is action research subsumed under the umbrella of reflective practice?
- Explain the terms *action* and *research* and how they may be connected within action research.
- Think of an action research project you are interested in conducting, follow the steps outlined above, and then consider what you have learned as a result.
- Gow, Kember, and McKay's (1996) study of action research in Hong Kong focused on attempts by teachers to encourage more independent student learning and reported improved student learning as a result of the action research project. You may want to read this article and see if you can replicate this project in your context and compare results.

Teaching Journals

Although I devote a separate chapter to teaching journals, I will briefly outline what they are here so that interested readers can go to that chapter for more details. When I first started reflecting on my teaching, I began writing a teaching journal. I was quite surprised at the patterns that emerged from my writing because I was actually cynical about the value of journaling on my teaching before I started. After a while, it came to the point that I actually enjoyed writing my reflective journal and looked forward to putting my ideas on paper because then I could *see* them. I outline this is more detail in the chapter that follows. Indeed, I have elsewhere (Farrell, 2007) suggested that writing regularly in a teaching journal can help teachers:

- gain awareness of their thinking;
- explore their own beliefs and practices;
- become more aware of their teaching styles; and
- better monitor their own practices. (Farrell, 2007, 2008b: 3)

That is what I experienced as I wrote for a while (6 months) and was able to see patterns develop in my thoughts that were now expressed through writing. This was a solo act, but teachers can also collaborate when they write about their practice and create a collaborative journal. Different from solo writing, collaborative journal writing with peers can be of value as peers add support and also can challenge each others' reflections. A collaborative teaching journal project was initiated in Hong Kong by Brock, Yu, and Wong (1992). They report on both the issues of writing with peers, such as trust and confidentiality issues, and the benefits, such as gaining different perspectives on their teaching that could not have been achieved by working alone. It is of interest to note that this group of teachers tended to tire of the exercise after a while, when the initial excitement began to diminish and the actual work of writing, meeting, and discussing their reflections began to eat into their limited time. As learned from this study, if entering into a collaborative journal writing relationship, it is prudent to set aside sufficient time before the group begins and to get a commitment from each member, from the outset, to continue with the activity until the agreed upon ending period.

Reflection Journal 2.9

First, write your own answers to these questions, and then find a partner or a group to discuss your findings and reflections; after these discussions in a pair or group, write a paragraph about your concluding reflections.

- Have you ever written a journal or diary of any kind (e.g. when you were young)?
- What is your understanding of a teaching journal?
- Start writing a journal about your teaching if you have not already started doing so. You can begin by reflecting on how and why you became a language teacher, if you do not have any other pressing matters you want to reflect on.
- Do you think you would be comfortable writing a collaborative teaching journal with a group of teachers?
- What might be important issues to discuss with the group before entering into such a collaborative teaching journal relationship?

Concept Mapping

Concept maps are visual representations of knowledge which show relationships between concepts in a type of network. Concept maps can be used by teachers to reflect; they can also be used to show how the learner is thinking about course content so as to evaluate what students know, and, more importantly, *how* they know what they know. Concept mapping can be used by individual language teachers to gauge their personal understandings of a particular topic, using the visual representations in a map to show how concepts or ideas are connected in their mind to any other concepts or ideas. As such, concepts and maps are a useful indication of what people know about a topic. Language teachers can also use concept maps with their students at the beginning of a new lesson in order to gauge how much their students have learned from previous lessons and/or to discuss any misunderstandings that may have occurred about the content of previous lessons. Thus, concept mapping allows language teachers to have a visual representation of the concepts they "see" as being important for a particular topic. As a result of this visualization, teachers can reflect on the meaning of concepts and how these maps represent their underlying beliefs about the topic in focus.

Reflection Journal 2.10

First, write your own answers to these questions, and then find a partner or a group to discuss your findings and reflections; after these discussions in a pair or group, write a paragraph about your concluding reflections.

- What is your understanding of a concept map?
- Have you even produced a concept map before?
- If not, try to construct a concept map of this chapter to aid you in your reflections. Was this helpful when you reflected?
- When educators use concept maps, they can change the manner of discourse in the class as they change the way they talk to their students, using words such as *think*, *classify*, *sequence*, *brainstorm*, and *reflect*. Students can in turn use these words to represent their cognitive processes. In other words, teachers not only teach content but also teach how to think about things such as how to classify, sequence, and reflect. Explain how you think this reflective process of using concept mapping might work with students in your classes.

Teacher Development Groups

In earlier work (Farrell, 2007; 2008b), I have suggested that "language teachers come together in teacher development groups to reflect so that they can complement each other's strengths and compensate for each other's limitations" (Farrell, 2008b: 3). Outcomes that may not be possible for an individual teacher working alone can be achieved by groups of teachers working together because a group can generate more perspectives and potential solutions than can any one person. Three types of teacher development groups can be noted:

peer groups within a specific school, teacher groups that operate outside a particular school but within a school district, and virtual groups formed on the Internet (Farrell, 2007; 2008b: 3). A valuable mode of teacher development involves study circles, in which teachers read and discuss research and then consider its implications for classroom and program practice (Farrell, 2008b). Such study groups offer teachers chances to focus and reflect, within a community of peers, on classroom content and methodologies. When teachers come together in a group to reflect, it is important that they all feel safe and trust each other (Farrell, 2004, 2007). They also need to commit to the group in terms of attendance, active participation, and the common good of all the group members. In addition, the group needs to allocate roles for each member, including that of group leader. I suggest a leadership arrangement of co-leaders, in which one person's role is to ensure that tasks are accomplished

Reflection Journal 2.11

First, write your own answers to these questions, and then find a partner or a group to discuss your findings and reflections; after these discussions in a pair or group, write a paragraph about your concluding reflections.

- List the various reasons why a group of language teachers would want to come together to talk about their teaching. Which of these purposes would be the easiest to pursue? Which would be the most time-consuming? Which would be the most likely to succeed, given the realities of a language teacher's busy schedule?
- What are the major factors to consider when forming a teacher development group? Rank these factors in order of importance.
- What do you think is the best method of attracting members to a teacher development group? If you have had experience in a teacher development group, how were you and other members recruited?
- Thinking about your own particular context now, how would you form a teacher development group and who would you ask to join you in this group?
- How many members should be in such a group?
- Which of the following roles (from Belbin, 1993) are most important to your group, and why?
  - *Coordinator* or *facilitator*, who makes a good chairperson and ensures that everyone in the group has an opportunity for input;
  - *Shaper*, who drives the group forward;
  - *Implementer*, who gets things done;
  - *Monitor or evaluator*, who ensures that all options are considered;
  - *Team worker*, who helps cement the group together;
  - *Resource investigator*, who develops outside contacts;
  - *Completer or finisher* who finishes things off;
  - *Expert*, who provides specific areas of knowledge.
- Can you think of other roles that would be suitable for a teacher group?

and the other person's role is to maintain group cohesion and personal relationships (Farrell, 2007; 2008b: 3–4). Trust is important in teacher development groups, to ensure that each member will be open and honest in discussions and will feel free to express his or her true opinions and feelings. For such trust to be established, group members must make a commitment that what is said in the group stays in the group. They must also commit to full involvement in all group meetings. When group members make this kind of strong commitment to their own and their colleagues' professional development, they can all grow professionally in their work (Farrell, 2007; 2008b: 2–3).

Classroom Observations

As noted in Farrell (2007), classrooms are busy places where a lot of things are happening at the same time. As a result, much of what is going on may remain largely unnoticed by the teacher. Classroom observations can help language teachers develop more of an awareness of what is really happening in their classes, what decisions they make, and why they make them. Classroom observation can be carried out alone, in pairs, and/or in small groups cross-observing each other's classes. Self-monitoring can be carried out through journal writing, self-reports, tally sheets, and/or recording (audio and video) lessons, with or without coding schemes to identify specific behaviors or practices. By later reviewing what is written or what is heard and seen on tape, aspects of teaching that may not have been obvious to the teacher during the class may become clearer (Farrell, 2007). However, this form of reflection may be limited as teachers may just focus on aspects of teaching they happen to see. They may therefore benefit by being challenged by a peer or critical friend who observes them teaching. When classroom observations are carried out with a peer or critical friend, they can also lead to more self-awareness about the type of teaching strategies other teachers use (Farrell, 2007).

In peer observations Richards and Lockhart (1994) recommend that when peers get together to observe each other's classes, they should incorporate pre-, during- and post-observation discussions. This should also be the format for groups wishing to engage in classroom observations (though it can be noted that discussions during observations may not always be possible). At the end of the observations, both pairs and groups can make use of Wallace and Woolger's (1991: 322) post-observation reflective questions:

- Establish the facts – What did the teacher do and what did the students do?
- What was achieved? What did the students learn?
- Seeking alternatives – What else could have been done?
- Self-evaluation – What have you learned?

The main point of classroom observations for the purposes of teacher development is that they are non-judgmental; for this to be the case, they must report the facts rather than what the observer thinks should have happened.

Reflection Journal 2.12

First, write your own answers to these questions, and then find a partner or a group to discuss your findings and reflections; after these discussions in a pair or group, write a paragraph about your concluding reflections.

- Have you ever been observed by others (apart from your students) while you were teaching? Who observed you, and why? Describe your experiences of being observed.
- Was your experience positive or negative? If positive, what made this classroom observation experience positive? If negative, what made this classroom observation negative?
- What can a teacher learn from observing another teacher teach a language class?
- What are the benefits of engaging in classroom observations with colleagues?
- What are things to look out for when engaging in classroom observations with colleagues, and why?

Teacher Metaphors

Lakoff and Johnson (1980: 232–233) suggest that a large part of self-understanding is the "search for appropriate personal metaphors that make sense of our lives…. The process of self-understanding is the continual development of new life stories for yourself." Teachers too use metaphors to describe what they do in their work. For example, they use metaphors to describe their teaching (e.g. teacher as "life-coach") or to describe their students (student as "clay to be molded"). They also use metaphors to describe their classroom (one teacher called it a "battlefield") and their work (one teacher noted that a teacher is an "octopus"). However, most teachers may not be aware of the impact of these images on their current teaching practices because they are implicit, often below the level of consciousness. It can be of value at some time during their careers for teachers to explore the images, metaphors, and maxims they have built up; as Burns (1999: 147) maintains, the metaphors that teachers hold can be used as "an introspective and reflective tool." Teaching metaphors are indications of the way teachers think about teaching and also guide the way they act in the classroom. When teachers begin to unpack the meaning of the metaphors they hold, they can begin to understand what they really believe about teaching and can start to change (internally as well as in terms of outward behavior) themselves as teachers.

Reflection Journal 2.13

First, write your own answers to these questions, and then find a partner or a group to discuss your findings and reflections; after these discussions in a pair or group, write a paragraph about your concluding reflections.

- What metaphor do you use for your role as a teacher? A teacher is "______"?
- Has your use of this metaphor changed over time since you became a language teacher?
- If yes, what differences have you noticed?
- What experiences have led to the change you noticed?
- If no changes have occurred in your metaphors for teaching, what experiences have resulted in this confirmation of your original metaphors?
- What metaphor do you use for the role of your students in your classes?
- What might be the result if your teaching metaphors and those of your students are different?
- Look at the following four teaching theories (Fox, 1983): the *transfer theory*, *shaping theory*, *traveling theory*, and *growing/changing theory*. Which one or more do you subscribe to, and why?
  - *Transfer Theory:* "The banking concept of education," in which the teacher knows all and transmits this knowledge to the students, who know nothing and passively learn;
  - *Shaping Theory:* The concept of teacher as a coach and as molding or modeling students into the proper (teacher-decided) shape;
  - *Traveling Theory:* Teachers and students exploring, travelling, collaborating, and learning together;
  - *Growth Theory:* Teachers lead learning through innovation and as agents of change.
- What metaphors do you use for your students? "A student is______?"
- Have these changed over the years? If so, how, and if not, why not?
- What metaphors do your students use for you as a teacher?
- What would you do if your students' metaphors are different from your metaphors for teaching and learning?

Teacher Maxims

A teacher's maxims help guide classroom behaviors and actions. Tsui (1995: 357) examined the personal maxims of two ESL teachers in the same Hong Kong secondary school and discovered two very different approaches to teaching the same subject, the same class, and the same proficiency level. One teacher, a Chinese female, was a strict disciplinarian and followed a *maxim of order* which was based on her cultural and educational background and which "valued subservience to authority and emphasized observation to protocol."

The other teacher, a New Zealander, encouraged a more informal relationship with his students; his classes were very different from those of the first teacher because of his Western cultural background. In the New Zealander's classes, as Tsui (1995: 359) pointed out, "more emphasis was placed on the individual, most classrooms had done away with the traditional protocol, and the relationship between students and teachers was much less formal." Teachers' maxims can thus be revealing as to how a teacher sees teaching and learning within his or her classroom.

Reflection Journal 2.14

First, write your own answers to these questions, and then find a partner or a group to discuss your findings and reflections; after these discussions in a pair or group, write a paragraph about your concluding reflections.

- What maxims do you use to describe your teaching?
- When you prepare your lessons, what is a maxim you could use to explain how you plan to teach that lesson?
- What maxims do you use to describe your students?
- What is your understanding of the following maxims (from Richards, 1998):
  - The maxim of *Accuracy*: work for accurate student output.
  - The maxim of *Efficiency*: make the most efficient use of class time.
  - The maxim of *Empowerment*: give the learners control.
  - The maxim of *Encouragement*: seek ways to encourage student learning.
  - The maxim of *Planning*: plan your teaching and try to follow your plan.
  - The maxim of *Involvement*: follow the learners' interests to maintain student involvement.
- Which of the above maxims do you agree with and use, and which do you disagree with and not use? Can you say why in each case?
- What maxims do you think your students use for your lessons, and why?

Teacher Beliefs

Teacher beliefs, those "unconsciously held assumptions about students, classrooms, and the academic material to be taught" (Kagan, 1992: 65), develop over a teacher's career and influence most classroom instructional decisions and actions. Knezedivc (2001:10) has suggested that awareness of beliefs and practices is a necessary starting point in reflections because we cannot develop "unless we are aware of who we are and what we do." As Knezedivc (2001: 10) further maintains, "developing awareness is a process of reducing the discrepancy between what we do and what we think we do." Language teachers must therefore, before being encouraged to make any changes, be given opportunities to be able to articulate their beliefs, what those beliefs mean to them, and whether they still remain valid in light of present-day research in teaching and learning. After articulating and reflecting on their beliefs about teaching and learning, language teachers can be encouraged to reflect on their actual classroom practices to see if there is alignment between their stated beliefs and their classroom practices. Because what teachers say they do and what they actually do in the classroom may not always the same, it is important for all teachers to test their stated beliefs against observations of classroom actions to see if there is any discrepancy between what they say and what they do.

Reflection Journal 2.15

First, write your own answers to these questions, and then find a partner or a group to discuss your findings and reflections; after these discussions in a pair or group, write a paragraph about your concluding reflections.

- The following questions may help you write a paragraph about your beliefs; read all the questions first and then write a paragraph.
  - What are your beliefs about language learning, and how do you think these relate to your teaching?
  - What are your beliefs about language teaching, and how do you think these relate to your teaching?
  - What is the source of your beliefs?
  - What is your role as a language teacher?
  - What do you think your students perceive to be your role as a language teacher?
  - Richards and Lockhart (1994: 3) have suggested that "teachers are often unaware of what they do when they teach." Do you agree or disagree with this statement? Why or why not?
  - Do your classroom practices reflect your stated beliefs about both language learning and language teaching? How do you know?

Critical Friendships

In a *critical friendship*, another person reflects with a teacher and gives advice as a trusted friend or colleague rather than a consultant, as a way to develop awareness of classroom events as well as the reflective abilities of the teacher who is conducting his or her own reflections. Such "critical friends" can give voice to a teacher's thinking like looking into a mirror, while at the same time being heard in a sympathetic but constructively critical way. As Hatton and Smith (1995) suggest, this challenging by the critical friend may be necessary for a deeper examination and evaluation of one's teaching. This type of reflection promotes collegiality and shared observations, but teachers should keep in mind that the focus is on the *friend* and not the *critical* in a trusting relationship.

Reflection Journal 2.16

First, write your own answers to these questions, and then find a partner or a group to discuss your findings and reflections; after these discussions in a pair or group, write a paragraph about your concluding reflections.

- What do critical friendships (in teaching or otherwise) mean to you?
- What would the benefits be if you entered into a critical friendship with a colleague rather than reflecting by yourself or with a group of teachers, and why?
- Do you think you can trust a colleague to become a critical friend?
- What problems do you think may occur with such friendships?
- What topics would you like to focus on for reflection with a critical friend that would be different from reflecting with a group of teachers?

Conceptions of Teaching

This section offers you an opportunity to reflect on your conceptions of teaching. In order to reflect in this way, you must write about your practice. Contained in this philosophy of teaching will be an examination of your values or your espoused theory of practice.

Teaching Values

A good place to begin examining your own teaching values is to look at the values currently being advocated by the field of second (or foreign) language teaching and to consider your relationship to these. Within the field of second language teaching, there are many competing theories (e.g. theories originating in second language acquisition, psychology, linguistics, education, and other fields) that espouse different values. Language teachers should be aware of these different orientations to the field so that they can consider if the theories which experts espouse are of value to them professionally. In order to examine teaching values, Freeman and Richards (1993) used a tripartite classification and suggested that conceptions of language teaching can fit the following categories: *science/research*, *theory/philosophy*, and *art/craft* conceptions; we can now use these as a template of sorts for examining language teaching values.

Science/Research Conceptions

Science/research conceptions of language teaching are guided from research and experimentation in second language education. For example, this conception of teaching looks to research that operationalizes learning principles, and teaching is seen as being influenced by psychological research on human memory and motivation. An example of this is *audiolingualism*, which developed out of research in behavioral psychology and which emphasizes stimulus-response-reinforcement with habit formation-learning drills in second language classes. As another example, second language acquisition research suggests that task-based learning with negotiation of meaning in the target language is more effective for language learners than some other approaches. Teaching which follows research findings can be seen as a scientifically based activity. This first orientation also promotes learner training, with researchers observing learners and asking about their learning strategies, based on the idea that we can teach effective learner strategies to all learners, especially the struggling learners. Also included in a science/research conception of teaching is research which documents and investigates specific teaching acts that are considered effective (a tested model based on student test results) and in which teaching is seen as an aggregate of these skills, such as effective teacher questioning, wait-time, grouping strategies, and the like. Hence, in this science/research conception, teaching the language effectively is seen as measurable and as a mirror of effective learning practices, which are also measurable.

Theory/Values Conceptions

The second major conception of teaching, focused on theory/values, is based on what ought to work or what is morally right in teaching. For example, if you follow this conception, you take it that teaching approaches are based not so much on what works but on what *should* work; or, in other words, based on rational thought and systematic reflection rather than experimentation. A good example of this is the ever popular approach of Communicative Language Teaching (CLT; Brumfit and Johnson, 1979) that was developed in reaction to the grammar-translation approach that preceded it. The CLT approach seeks to operationalize a theory of "communicative competence" (a term coined by Hymes, 1966) and is philosophical rather than empirical in that much of the discussion about its value is based on how effective many teachers (especially those coming from Western teaching traditions) believe it should be, based on its properties of focusing on communication rather than language *per* se. (And indeed, research on CLT has produced decidedly mixed results.) Also, and from an earlier time in our methodology, the Silent Way (Gattegno, 1972) fits into this conception of teaching, in which students were encouraged not to speak until they felt ready to, based on the belief that this initially "silent approach" would help them develop perception first as a basis for their speaking later. While it seems that such an approach might be of value, it conflicts with other views of how best to teach.

Educators who follow this particular conception of teaching see scientifically based approaches as being too narrow, and they suggest that their individual classroom success provides enough justification (some even call this "empirical verification"). Another possibility within this conception of teaching is subscribing to a more politically focused model that is based on values one holds for teachers, learners, classrooms, and the overall role of education in society. The general aim of teaching in this conceptual model is to promote particular values that are usually political. Humanistic approaches, which are concerned with the affective side of language learning and which emphasize human values in language teaching, fall under this umbrella as do learner-centered approaches which are applied based on a sense of teaching out of respect for individual needs and differences. An example is Community Language Learning, or Counseling-Learning (CLL) (Curran, 1972), an approach in which the teacher takes on the role of a language counselor who leads students to overcome their language learning fears (see Stevick, 1980, for discussion and implementation of this method). If you value team-teaching as an approach, then you are also likely to see collaboration as an important value.

Reflection Journal 2.17

First, write your own answers to these questions, and then find a partner or a group to discuss your findings and reflections; after these discussions in a pair or group, write a paragraph about your concluding reflections.

- Freeman and Richards (1993) sum up the three different conceptions as follows:
  - Science/Research conceptions suggest ready-made specific solutions;
  - Theory/Values conceptions suggest ready-made general solutions; and
  - Art/Craft conceptions suggest custom- and self-made solutions.

  Which of these seems closest to your conception of teaching?
- The key to exploring and examining your teaching values is that once you have reflected on your conceptions of teaching, you then begin to examine them more closely by asking yourself which of the values that the profession puts forth you embrace. Are there any inconsistencies between your personal values and those of your profession? These now become issues and points at which to begin conversations and dialogue among colleagues and within the profession (at large).
- Once you have reflected on what you hold to be important within your professional practice, it's time to articulate these values. The following exercise may prove helpful:
  - Imagine you are writing to a colleague, someone with whom you feel very comfortable. You want to communicate about your professional practice so that your colleague will understand how you carry out your professional work and what is most important to your professional practice. Take one to two pages to complete this exercise. (adapted from Hunt, 1980)

Art/Craft Conceptions

The third conception, that of art or craft, is based on an individual teacher's skill and personality, not on any particular system or method of teaching, and so is in contrast to the first two conceptions described above. In this conception, teaching depends on the individual teacher, and not the form of teaching. From an art/craft perspective, a good teacher might see a range of options available to him or her after carefully analyzing a classroom situation, and then is able to select the one that is likely to be most effective for teaching within the particular context. Responsibility lies with the individual teacher to know what is available but at the same time does not commit the teacher to any one method of teaching in all situations. Within this art/craft conception, teachers can explore their teaching in a systematic way so that they become informed decision makers and thus are responsible for what occurs in their classrooms (Farrell, 2007).

Reflecting on Teaching Philosophy

Now that you have reflected on what you consider important in terms of professional values with respect to the different conceptions and values of the language teaching profession, you can start reflecting on specific aspects of your practice that are important to you. You are now ready to write your teaching philosophy, a summary of your beliefs that guide your professional practice.

Reflection Journal 2.18

First, write your own answers to these questions, and then find a partner or a group to discuss your findings and reflections; after these discussions in a pair or group, write a paragraph about your concluding reflections.

- Here are some more reflections that can help you while you are writing your teaching philosophy:
  - What do I think about the language I am teaching?
  - What are my beliefs about language teaching?
  - How do these beliefs influence my teaching?
  - Where do my beliefs come from?
  - What way or ways do I teach in the classroom?
  - How do I know what I do?
  - What is my role as a language teacher?
  - How does my sense of my role contribute to my teaching style?
  - What do my learners believe about language learning?
  - What do my learners believe about my role as a teacher and my teaching?
  - How do these beliefs influence their approach to learning?
  - What learning strategies do my learners adopt?
  - What learning styles do my learners favor?

This teaching philosophy is an official statement that should be no more than two pages long. Osterman and Kottkamp (1993) recommend organizing your statement under the following useful five headings:

- *Aims of professional work*
- *Goals for students*
- *Goals for self*
- *Preferred student/teacher relationship*
- *Preferred work climate.*

After you have written your teaching philosophy, you can compare your philosophy to what you actually do in your classroom. When you start writing your philosophy of practice, you will realize that you are actually asking yourself what you do, why you do it, what the result is, and whether you will continue in the same way now that you have answered the previous questions. This is the starting point in reflecting on your practice.

A Brief Caution

My discussion of reflective practice and the various forms and activities associated with reflection that I have presented in this chapter may seem to paint a rosy picture of reflective practice and all that it entails. This is usually the case when I talk about reflective practices; yet there are situations that teachers must be aware of when considering reflecting on their practice. The first major issue is that you must be *ready* to reflect. This means you must be in a state of mind that welcomes questions and criticisms of practice which you may have been following for many years but have not really stopped long enough to question. Intuition is generally a guide, but it can also lead teachers astray when they reach sensitive areas in their lives. Reflective practice usually spills over into teachers' non-professional lives too as they consider why they became teachers in the first place.

Another issue teachers should be aware of is their preferred mode of reflection. This book is mainly about writing in various different forms as a means of reflective practice. However, I am well aware that not all teachers (or other individuals), even though they may be fluent writers, like writing or are comfortable with writing as a mode of reflective practice. Indeed, some teachers may prefer speaking in a teacher development group (see above), talking with a critical friend (see above), or just reflecting on their own. I recognize this and would not force anybody to write if they were not comfortable with it as a mode of reflection. That said, there is technology available now whereby one can speak into a microphone, with software that can turn the spoken word into text, and this may be a way for some to overcome their reluctance to write.

Reflection Journal 2.19

First, write your own answers to these questions, and then find a partner or a group to discuss your findings and reflections; after these discussions in a pair or group, write a paragraph about your concluding reflections.

- Here are some questions for reflection that really get to the core of reflective practice and you as a teacher. I caution you, however, that some of these questions may get under your skin and delve into topics that you may not have entertained for many years, if ever. If you can get through these questions, you should be ready for the remainder of the book, so please do try.
  - Do you ever feel helpless about your teaching situation and your role as a teacher? If so, why?
  - Do you think that you are working as a teacher in an impersonal education system? If so, what can you do about this?
  - Why did you become a teacher?
  - Did you really want to become a teacher? Why or why not?
  - If you were not a teacher, what do you think you would have liked to have done instead?
  - Do you agree or disagree with the following statement: "Those that can, do; those that can't, teach." Explain your answer.
  - Define what the word *teacher* means to you.
  - Have you ever experienced a feeling of being "burned out" from teaching? Describe these feelings.
  - If yes, can you outline what you think caused the burnout?
  - How did you overcome the feeling of burnout (assuming you have overcome this)?
  - Why do you think anyone would leave the teaching profession because of burnout or for any other reason?
  - Do you personally know any teachers who have quit the profession? If so, why did they say they were leaving teaching?
  - Do you know how you can take more control of your teaching situation?
  - Do you think reflecting on your teaching (both inside and outside the classroom) can help you take more control of your teaching life? If so, how?
  - What is the most frightening aspect of reflective practice for you, and why?
  - If you discovered that you really did not like teaching after reading this book and engaging in intensive reflective practice, would you consider giving up teaching?
  - If you decided to give up teaching, what do you think you would do, and why?
  - How would you advise novice teachers who are just about to graduate from their teacher education or other graduate program? What should they avoid in their first year? What should they look forward to? What should they expect?
  - How will you consider your professional development from now on?

Whatever your mode of reflection, I think just reading the contents of this book, even without any written reflections, may be a useful reflective exercise for most teachers – at least, I hope it is!

Conclusion

Reflective practice can mean different things to different educators, but regardless how one defines it, most agree that some form of reflection is desirable for all teachers. If teachers blindly follow routine without any reflection, they are heading for burnout, not to mention that they are doing a disservice to their students. Reflective practice gives teachers options when deciding what to do in their classrooms. Reflective practice helps teachers avoid burnout and routine approaches to their teaching and life in general because reflection is a way of being or a state of mind that guides actions. There are many different ways teachers can reflect on their work, and all of these methods have advantages along with some disadvantages. It is up to each individual teacher or teacher group to decide which method would be most beneficial, depending on the purposes of their reflections. Most of all, reflective practice enables teachers to make more informed decisions about their teaching, and, as a result, their students receive the best possible opportunities for reaching success in their learning.

Chapter 2 Reflections

First, write your own answers to these questions, and then find a partner or a group to discuss your findings and reflections; after these discussions in a pair or group, write a paragraph about your concluding reflections after reading this chapter.

- How can reflection help teachers make sense of their work?
- What kinds of reflective activities can help teachers reflect?
- Which of the following reflective activities would suit you:
  - Action research
  - Concept mapping
  - Teaching journals
  - Teacher groups
  - Classroom observations
  - Teacher metaphors
  - Teacher maxims
  - Teacher beliefs
  - Critical friends
- Describe the advantages and disadvantages of each of the above activities.
- Can you think of any other reflective activities that would be suitable for language teachers to use for their reflections on practice?

3. Writing as Reflective Practice

Preamble

I must say that I always hated writing in school because I felt that I was being constrained in some way, and anyway, I could not spell. In those days, we did not have computers to alert us to spelling errors or indeed, grammar errors, and I could not understand why I was not allowed to write the way I spoke. One day, I got excited after I had read the book, *Moby Dick*, as the start of this book really impressed me as to how the scene was set. Over time, I slowly became more interested in reading. The next time I realized the difference between the written word and the spoken word was when I saw a movie and then read the book that the movie was based on. I realized then that the movie could not capture the written word and that the book had so much more for my imagination to play with. I remember thinking that as I read I could see the characters and the context much more clearly than when I watched the movie made from the book. However, I still was not willing to sit down and write because I did not know anything about paragraphs, sentences, or words and so could not choose these in any correct manner as I wrote. I therefore became frustrated every time I had to write an essay in class.

On reflection, I realize that I was not planning my writing and all that involves. It is quite possible that my high school teachers tried their best to convey the conventions of writing in class – I don't really remember; I may have tuned out by that time. The essays I wrote in high school were always returned with so many red marks outlining mistakes in grammar, spelling, and/or writing conventions that it seemed the color of the essay had changed from black to red on the pages. I cannot remember one comment on my essay that praised any ideas I had tried to write regardless of their awkward wording, spelling, or grammar. I think my teachers just went after the mistakes (and, no doubt, there were many); they forgot to look for meaning and what I was trying to say. I do not remember anybody teaching me how to write, but I do remember all of my teachers testing my writing abilities (and grammar knowledge) frequently. Perhaps this is where I got my mantra as a teacher: "I am a teacher, not a tester," in that I always try to make sure I teach before I test. When a teacher asks you to answer the 10 questions that follow a reading passage, this is testing, so I assume the same teacher has shown his or her students how to look for the answers of these questions in previous classes. In my day, exams had already hijacked the education system: all anyone was interested in was what grade you got (and mine were not that high), rather than what you learned. It was not until my university days that I learned how to write, but again, nobody showed me; I just picked it up to survive. It was in my graduate school days that I really learned all about writing, when I had to take courses on how to teach second language writing and also had to be able to publish some of my own writing if I wanted to succeed as an academic.

Reflection Journal 3.1

First, write your own answers to these questions, and then find a partner or a group to discuss your findings and reflections; after these discussions in a pair or group, write a paragraph about your concluding reflections.

- What do you remember about your early days in grade school as a writer?
- Did you like to write?
- Did your friends like to write?
- Did you write for fun (e.g. in a diary)?
- What do you remember about your writing instruction (if you got any)?
- How did your teacher "correct" your writing?
- Was your teacher a tester or a teacher of writing?
- How did your teacher "teach" writing?
- Would you say your experiences of writing in school tended to encourage you to continue writing or to discourage you?
- What activities and experiences tended to encourage you to write?
- What activities and experiences tended to discourage you from writing?
- If you were a parent with a young child, how you would excite your child about the joys of writing (or would you)?

Why Write?

Why write at all is what I was thinking when my teacher admonished me about my failures in essay writing. What is the point of writing when it is possible to say a lot more and a lot faster, too, by talking? I had no idea why I should even bother with writing, as it seemed to me to be too time-consuming. In fact, I would probably say that the only real reason I became a writer in the first place was that I was forced to write while I was in graduate school, where a key mode of learning and communication between professor and students (in both reading and writing) is through the written word. So as a graduate student, I had to learn how to write; but I did not realize for a while that much of the time a person takes to write is actually taken up with trying to organize thoughts and to find the words to express them on paper. In contrast, when speaking, organization is much looser and ideas are not so precise. When writing, a person must pause for a short time (how long depends on each individual) in order to organize thoughts somewhat before putting them on paper, using a pen or pencil or writing directly into a computer as a word processor. This *pausing* is the first step in reflective writing because it is the launching pad for what is to follow. When people talk, most just say what is on their mind within reason and with a slight bit of prior thought, although there are people who, as we all know, do not think at all before they speak. Speaking is typically relatively instantaneous and interactive with another person or persons (unless, of course, the speaker is engaged in a monolog). It is much easier to say something spontaneously than it is to write something spontaneously because we cannot see the words we speak and therefore do not even consider how they are spelled, not to mention how or whether they would form a sentence. Speaking does not in fact require so-called complete sentences; if you are looking for examples of real spontaneous speech, just listen to interviews of native speakers on news shows, few of whom speak in complete sentences or "correct" grammar and some of whom may even sound incoherent.

The time needed to write is a natural check on these tendencies of spontaneous speech. The act of writing (as reflective practice) has a built-in reflective mechanism that makes it an ideal tool for helping teachers pause and thus engage in systematic reflections of their practice. This chapter outlines the process of writing and how personal reflective writing can help teachers gain an understanding of themselves as professionals. The chapter begins with a

Reflection Journal 3.2

First, write your own answers to these questions, and then find a partner or a group to discuss your findings and reflections; after these discussions in a pair or group, write a paragraph about your concluding reflections.

- What is writing to you at this stage of your life?
- Do you like to write? If yes, why? If not, why not?
- Do you write often? If yes, what kind of writing do you do?
- Who do you write to? Why?
- Does pausing help you organize your thoughts before you put them on paper or do you avoid this and jump into your writing without thinking or planning first?
- Do you think there is one correct way to write and that everyone should follow this way of writing?

brief outline of how I started reflecting on practice by engaging in one of my largest writing ventures, my own Ph.D. dissertation. This is then followed by a discussion of how teachers can write to help them reflect on their practice.

Autobiographical: Personal Reflective Writing

Writing to Know

When writers reflect on their own professional journey and experiences, this is sometimes called *autobiographical writing*, and it usually takes the form of a narrative text. These autobiographical narrative texts are teachers' subjective perceptions about particular events that occur in their professional lives and therefore provide unique teacher-generated insight without any input or interference from outside researchers. But how does one start on these autobiographical writing journeys?

I have a somewhat unique story about how I started; it begins with the slogan: "How do I know what I think until I see what I say?" This saying from E. M. Forster (Forster (1966/1927) has always guided my own personal reflective writing. I find that my head is sometimes filled with all sorts of thoughts feverishly moving around in tangled clumps of intertwining messages that sometimes are too fast for me to consider separately or even consider at all. In order to capture and slow down these thoughts, I discovered that the act of writing them down (on paper or word-processed) enabled me to control the mind a bit and get some order into what these thoughts all mean to me. It was not an easy process at first, but I discovered that this writing process enabled me to step back for a moment to consider the thoughts that were now written down and visible, a reflective process that was next to impossible as those same thoughts spun around in my head. By writing down my ideas, I was able to get control of my own thinking, and as a result I could direct my reflections more and even my future actions. It was later that I read the saying from E. M. Forester; but when I did, I realized that this was in fact what I was doing all along. That said, I was still very unsure about what I was writing and whether it was following the proper conventions. For example, I was not sure if I should write perfect sentences from the very beginning, with correct spelling and perfect organization, or how many drafts I should write. I also remember thinking that the number of drafts necessary was probably a direct indication of the poor quality of the writing: the more drafts required, the lower the quality of the writing. That was until I saw copies of the famous American author, E. B. White's rough drafts in a writing textbook when I was in school. These amazed me because he had crossed out whole sentences and extensively changed the words on many pages of the drafts. Now, this drafting process was beginning to suit my own personality as a writer. I discovered that I could rewrite drafts rather than just come up with one draft that had to be perfect in every way from the outset. Unfortunately, some of my own graduate students still think this is the correct way to write as they hand in one and only one draft although I also assume they do not have the time (or interest?) to write multiple drafts – but that is a topic for another forum. In sum, I was beginning to find my own way of writing by "seeing" my thoughts in written form, and this then began to help me make sense of what I was thinking.

Reflection Journal 3.3

First, write your own answers to these questions, and then find a partner or a group to discuss your findings and reflections; after these discussions in a pair or group, write a paragraph about your concluding reflections.

- What is your understanding of "How do I know what I think until I see what I say?"
- Do you know what you think before you write?
- What would your slogan be for getting the written word on paper (or computer)?
- Do you use outlines before you begin to write?
- Are you a "thinker" – you think a lot before you put your first word on paper?
- Are you a "jumper" – you go straight into the act of writing from the very beginning?
- Do you have a different and more personal way of beginning your writing?
- Do you think you can make your writing correct from the first draft?
- Why would you or would you not want to write multiple drafts?
- Why do you think professional writers write many drafts?

I now present an autobiographical narrative on my own reflections of how I started reflective writing and how I used reflective writing to gain personal insight into my professional journey.

My Beginnings

I started my own reflections on my practice in 1984 by writing frequently in a teaching journal (see following chapter for details on teaching journals). I must say that from the outset, I was skeptical not only about the whole idea of reflective practice, but also about how any teacher could actually do (read: perform) this thing called reflection. My only earlier encounters with reflection were through meditation, but I found that difficult because so many other ideas came rushing into my head as I sat and attempted to reflect. This was before I had started teaching and before I called myself a teacher. After completing my Bachelor's degree, I studied for a Higher Diploma in Education (H. Dip. in Ed.) and became a teacher. After teaching in Ireland and after several years teaching ESL in Korea, I began to wonder about my teaching and about being a teacher. I agree with Palmer (1998: 5), who encourages all teachers to "ask the 'who' question – 'who is the self that teaches?'" This question was an important element in my introduction to the concept of reflective practice.

Key work that influenced my thinking was that of John Fanselow (Fanselow, 1987, 1988). Fanselow takes the approach that teachers should be responsible for their own classrooms, and thus he encourages teachers to explore their classroom practice from the point of view of analyzing the communication patterns that occur in it. My own reflective curiosity, set off initially by Fanselow's work, brought me back to graduate school in the United States in pursuit of a Ph.D. This intense period of reflection led me to write a dissertation on the topic of reflective practice (Farrell, 1996). This means that the main tool for my reflective dissertation was reflecting through writing. A very influential person for me academically at that time was Dan Tannacito, my first professor in the Ph.D. course. During that period, I noticed that Dr. Tannacito had a keen insight not only into his subject matter of Applied Linguistics, but also into those he was teaching, the students: he always knew how to deal with a somewhat delicate balance from one group of students to another group, considering that each group included many international students with very different cultural backgrounds. His classroom delivery was Socratic and made each student dig deep into his or her own experiences to bring out the best in each of them. I still remember Dr. Tannacito telling me in his Second Language Acquisition course in the summer of 1993 that writing was the means to look at the writer. This is yet another insight that fed my thinking about reflective practice.

One day, when I was reading for one of my classes, I saw the term for the first time and was smitten immediately because these two words, *reflective practice*, articulated exactly and succinctly why I was in a Ph.D. program in the first place. Finally, I was beginning to grasp what had made me move half way across the globe with my family: to explore and examine the meaning of what I was doing professionally. This realization kept me going throughout the program (anyone who has completed a Ph.D. program knows that completing it sometimes has as much to do with stamina as intellectual ability). The coursework and the reading for my oral and written examinations to be allowed start a dissertation became very enjoyable after that, especially the reading and study for my oral exams, because everything I was doing began to slowly come together in terms of a focus that was to influence the choice of topic I made for my dissertation.

Dissertation Research

Choosing a topic for my dissertation thus was not difficult for me anymore because I had embarked on a reflective journey a few years before by signing up for a Ph.D. program at Indiana University of Pennsylvania (IUP), in the United States. During the coursework, I found myself reflecting on and trying to interpret my teaching practices and the practices of other teachers I had observed informally while a teacher in Korea during the previous 15 years. I began to conceptualize where my philosophy of language education had originated, how it was crystallizing during the program, and its impact on the new information I was picking up in the various courses I was taking. It was all very exciting for me and more so because I had discovered that there was an actual subfield in Education and other fields (e.g. Medicine) called Reflective Practice. So I read voraciously on this "new" topic (of course, I discovered that it was not "new" to the Education field – see the work of John Dewey, e.g. Dewey, 1933), and my reflections began to take some shape. Another very influential teacher for me at IUP at that time was Jerry Gebhard, who became my thesis supervisor because of the type of reflective work he was researching (e.g. Gebhard, 1992). It was at that same time that I was also being influenced by the work of Dr. Gebhard's mentor, John Fanselow (as introduced above).

So my dissertation topic was set, a qualitative study that looked at a small group of English as a foreign language (EFL) teachers in Korea as they reflected on their work. Specifically, the study described and analyzed the content of reflection, what the participants wrote about and talked about at group meetings and individually when they reflected on their work; the type and level of reflection, whether critical or descriptive; and the development of critical reflection from the start to the end of the research. During the reflective process, I was not only a facilitator for the project, but I also attempted to guide the teachers through the reflective process by talking about methods of classroom observation they could employ as well as guiding the initial discussions during the group meetings until they had decided on how they wanted to reflect. Thus, to a certain extent, I also functioned as an "outside expert" as I guided them through the process.

My research used ethnographic methods of data collection and analysis. Data were collected through my researcher's log, group discussions, participants' journal writing, individual discussions with teachers, classroom observations, and the collection of various written artifacts. The findings indicated that when the participants reflected at the group meetings and wrote in their journals, they were reflecting at a very descriptive level; it was only in the individual discussions that the participants reflected on a more critical level, though this was not true for all of the participants. At the time (Farrell, 1996), I proposed a model for the professional self-development of EFL teachers composed of the following five core components:

- A variety of opportunities for teachers to reflect through a range of different activities;
- Built-in ground rules for the reflection process and for each activity;
- Four different types of time;
- Input from external sources; and
- Low affective states.

These are explained briefly below.

A variety of opportunities for teachers to reflect through a range of different activities. A variety of reflective activities can be done alone or together with others, as teachers can select just one of the activities, a combination of activities, or all of them to perform. I suggest any, or all, of the following activities, which the Korean group performed: (a) group discussions, (b) class observations (self/pair/group), and (c) journal writing (self/pair/group).

Built-in ground rules for the reflection process and for each activity. There should be a negotiated set of agreed rules or guidelines that each group or pair follows in order to keep everyone focused and the reflective process running smoothly. For example, a group will have to decide who will chair the meetings. I suggest a revolving chair, with a resulting revolving level of responsibility for individual group members, to provide a site for meeting and refreshments and to make the agenda of the meetings. This chairperson should also be willing to use his or her position to protect and encourage the free expression of views. For observations, certain understandings need to be negotiated ahead of time. For example, what are the responsibilities of the observer? Is intervention by the observer possible or desirable in the class? Will the class be videotaped, audiotaped, or neither? If you make a tape, how will this be analyzed, and for what purposes or desired outcomes? What is to be observed, and how is the observation to be carried out?

Four different types of time. For practicing teachers to be able to reflect on their work, time is a very important consideration. I suggest that four different views and types of time be incorporated as follows:

- Individual time: a certain level of time commitment by each participant should be negotiated by the group at the start of the process;
- Time of each activity: decide on how much time should be spent on each reflective activity;
- Time needed to develop reflection: this activity cannot be done quickly and only progresses when individual teachers are ready to reflect;
- Time frames for the period of reflection: decide on how long the reflective process should last.

Input from external sources. See what others are saying about teaching, such as comments from colleagues and what is written in professional journals, books, and teaching magazines. This is important, as teachers need to compare what they see and do in their own teaching with what others see and do in their teaching; otherwise, they will merely emphasize their own personal experiences, which may inhibit the likelihood of making any changes.

Low affective states. The above four components of the model all pose some threat and associated anxiety for practicing teachers. For all participants to grow together as teachers, it is important that trust develops naturally from people caring about each other as individuals and as a group or a pair. Thus, establishing a supportive attitude will help to ensure a positive atmosphere and a low affective state of calmness and relaxation that encourages openness and honest reflection.

Following the mentorship from Jerry Gebhard and my knowledge of his research (e.g. Gebhard, 1992), I became aware of the importance of reflecting on the participants' views and how my own preconceptions can color an issue, so I and others who reflect must be also aware of the setting and its impact on the participants' viewpoints.

Using Reflection to Gain Perspective

As Lofland and Lofland (1984: 119–120) point out, "Reflection is a transformation of self during the qualitative process" and can lead to..."a redefinition of values" so that..."you are not the person you were when you began." I am certainly not now nor was I then, when I defended the dissertation after writing it, the same person as I was when the project began. In fact, I encountered some changes right at the beginning of the dissertation process, as I know because I recorded all of my personal feelings in my log, under the title "hunches," in the form of writing a memo to myself. I found this a very useful method to keep track of my own feelings and changes. I now outline the changes and problems I encountered in writing and researching on this topic of reflective practice.

One important issue I faced was about whether I should "push" the participants or not during the study. By "push" I meant enforcing my suggestions as to the direction the group should go when investigating their teaching, rather than letting them go their own way; I wondered what would happen for example if I "pushed" them when they were not ready to be pushed or wanted to go a different way? Thus, as a participant-observer, I faced a classic dilemma reflected in the following statement by Hornberger (1994: 69):

> The dilemma is over how to strike a balance between insider and outsider perspectives.... [T]oo much participation by the

> researcher may change the course of action of the culture, classroom, or event being studied but too little participation may miss the course of action altogether.

I tried to balance my participation with the idea that my knowledge and experience was different from that of the other participants. As I looked at my notes and transcripts of the first few meetings, I realized that I was the initiator of most of the communication in the group meetings. The meetings were thus becoming too *me-directed*, and I realized that I might be blocking opportunities for others to talk and reflect on their work. Therefore, I decided not to be the originator of much of the communication from then on. Also, I decided not to intervene if the other participants were silent. On reflection, I would say that my role as participant-observer was challenging because I was always aware of the necessity of striking the balance between my role as researcher and that of facilitator of the other teachers' reflections (throughout the process I did not in fact reflect on my own teaching).

I experienced many other dilemmas as I was writing my dissertation, not the least of which was how to manage such a long document (65,000 words, approximately); however, the benefits of this writing experience has served me well over the years. Ringing loud in my ears are the words of Jersild (1955: 82), who asserts that "to help a pupil to have meaningful experiences, a teacher must know the pupil as a person. This means that the teacher must strive to know himself." It is not easy to know where to start when trying to know yourself as a teacher and as a person. Nias (1987: 140) has pointed out that teachers have a sense of personal identity which "transcends their choice of an occupational identity, that is, they see themselves as 'me' first and 'teacher' second." They will try to maintain a sense of fit between occupational and personal identity to "be themselves" in the classroom (Nias, 1987). Nias continues:

> There is compelling evidence that all changes in personal identity involve feelings of loss, anxiety and conflict. During any redefinition of self, people struggle with doubt and pain. Personal change, it appears, is always accompanied by a sense of losing control; the more fundamental the shift, the deeper and more traumatic the uncertainty and the greater the need for reassurance and support. Alterations in occupational identity have a similar effect.
>
> (Nias, 1987: 141)

Engaging in reflective practice can result in some pain and anxiety as one reflects. However, if teachers can recognize this and can live with the ambiguity of not knowing the result of the reflective process while they are involved in it, while still maintaining trust in themselves, it can be a powerful experience for all involved, as members of the first group of teachers I worked with have attested to (Farrell, 1996). The three teachers, the participants in the group, felt empowered as a result of the experience and learned to accept this and continue with the process of their own self-development.

Reflection for me became a powerful tool to help me look at my teaching beliefs and compare these to what I was actually doing in the classroom. When I observed the other teachers in the group, I was able to reflect on my own teaching; I found Fanselow's (1988: 2) ideas useful for remembering that we see our own teaching in the teaching of others, and I could use these observations as "a mirror so that I could see that what [another teacher was] doing is a reflection of much of what I do." When I wrote many kinds of reflections in my dissertation, read and reread them then and now 15 years later, I see the power of writing as reflective practice and the real meaning of "How do I know what I think until I see what I say?"

Reflection Journal 3.4

First, write your own answers to these questions, and then find a partner or a group to discuss your findings and reflections; after these discussions in a pair or group, write a paragraph about your concluding reflections.

- As you were reading my experiences and reflections on my writing, what was your reaction?
- Do you think writing is a useful tool for reflecting on your personal and professional life?
- How do you begin your writing regardless of what you write?
  - Do you use a pen and paper or a computer?
  - Do you write immediately whatever comes into your head?
  - Do you wait until you get clear ideas and thoughts before you put anything on paper?
  - Do you, for example, write an outline, draw a picture of your thoughts, write everything that comes into your head for a fixed period of time, or have some other way of starting?
  - Do you agonize about what to write for some time before getting anything on paper?
  - Do you always need to have correct sentence structure and grammar from the very first moment you start writing?
  - Do you have to have an organized paragraph or paragraphs from the very first moment you begin your writing?
  - Do you not care about organization, sentence structure and punctuation when you first write and just put it down any way it comes out?
  - What is your approach to grammar in writing? Do you worry about this from the beginning, at a second draft stage, or at the end of your writing process?

What is Writing?

Generally, people use oral language (talk) in order to communicate with each other, whether they want to exchange information or just to chat in a friendly way about nothing in particular such as the weather. They may want to exchange information about something specific with one or more people, or they may want to keep socially active by exchanging pleasantries with friends, neighbors, or working colleagues. It is possible to accomplish the same communication by writing to people, but this is generally (other than perhaps when texting) more deliberate and a more formal type of communication because there is a *time gap* between when a person first gets an idea and when he or she actually communicates that idea by writing it for others to read. In addition, when we write we must follow certain conventions such as using upper case or capital letters at the beginning of a sentence, certain punctuation, correct grammar, and usually also full sentences. These conventions add another dimension to language use, in that it is necessary to separate ideas and thoughts from how these are presented in writing and to follow conventions that are generally not applicable to speaking. Hence, one can hear comments such as, "She just blurted that out," referring to an utterance in which the speaker seems to say exactly what she is thinking. People get away with this without too much trouble or any trouble at all, because everyone knows that speech is unplanned and almost anything can come out of a speaker's mouth. Writing, on the other hand, in being a more deliberate form of communication, means that a writer should be more careful how communication is presented because there will be a lasting record of it. Why then do people write rather than speak if they must take all of this care and extra time by following writing conventions, using correct grammar, and being aware that they are leaving a permanent record of their thoughts?

People write for many different purposes; many realize that they are leaving a record of their thoughts and as such plan carefully what and where they write because someone is going to read what has been written. Many people learn to write in school for the first time and use writing for academic purposes such as completing a term paper or an essay or taking notes in a class. Outside of school, people write in their jobs and to communicate to each other either formally or informally, such as writing a letter, an email, or a text message to a friend. Consequently, the audience for a piece of writing is very important because the writer hopes to influence the intended audience. In school, many students quickly learn that the main audience for an assigned piece of writing such as an essay is the teacher, whereas community members or the general public will be the main audience for a letter written and published in a local newspaper. A scholar who writes for a specific academic journal will have in mind as audience a certain group of academics who tend to read such journals and so will pitch the writing style and content to that audience and to the writing conventions expected in such a journal. Thus, the purpose and audience will influence the style of writing, which can take the form of formal academic or professional writing style or of a more informal style such as in letter writing, texting, or electronic mail communications.

Reflection Journal 3.5

First, write your own answers to these questions, and then find a partner or a group to discuss your findings and reflections; after these discussions in a pair or group, write a paragraph about your concluding reflections.

- When you write, what is the most difficult aspect of the writing process?
- How do you end your written piece? Do you just finish and not look at it again? Do you reread and change many things? Or do you give it to someone else to read and comment?
- Do you read over your writing or just leave it? Do you have a difficult time reading your own writing, or do you read over it again and again because you are not satisfied with it?
- Do you ever ask others to read your writing, or are you apprehensive about letting them look at your writing?
- Have you ever published any of your writing?

Writing: Product or Process?

What I am going to present next can be seen as an oversimplification of the act of writing, but I want to keep our discussion general for the benefit of those who may not have much experience either writing or talking about writing. I also want the discussion to encourage you to write by first defining your own philosophy of writing. In order to do this, I have divided the act of writing into two main views (I am aware that there are many more views) – writing as a *product* and writing as a *process* – so that each teacher can decide where he or she places himself or herself along a continuum with *product* and *process* on opposite ends (see Figure 3.1 below). The discussion that follows is taken from the perspective of how teachers of second or foreign languages use these approaches to teaching writing to their students.

Product ————————————	**Process**
(An Object)	(An Activity)

Figure 3.1 The continuum of writing.

Product

Writing viewed as *product* suggests that writers produce accurate pieces of written text or compositions and that this product reflects the author's competence as a writer. Teachers emphasize grammar and vocabulary and teach them overtly in a product-oriented writing class, assuming that this instruction will help students write clearly in a second or foreign language. The teachers provide models of good writing for their students to follow so that they can avoid errors; but if they do make errors, the teacher will correct these while all the time emphasizing accurate grammar, correct sentence structure, spelling, punctuation, and writing structures. In a product approach, the content of the writing is not as important as the mechanics because the goal of teaching writing is to teach students to produce replicas of the types of texts they will most encounter in their lives: persuasive writing, argumentative writing, narratives, expository writing, and other genres.

One of the main problems with this approach is that it focuses on accuracy in grammar and structure while overlooking the process of writing itself, including the strategies the students used in getting to the final draft. In other words, if students make mistakes, they do not realize why they made them; and, in many cases, they continue to make many of the same mistakes over and over again. Additionally, the writing process is very much controlled from beginning to end, and thus students are "stuck" within only those models and structures they have been taught. They do not learn how to create their own individual pieces of writing.

Process

This book emphasizes a strategic approach to teaching of all the skill areas. Within this orientation, there exists an alternative approach, the *process approach*, which considers how people develop a piece of writing from the beginning to the end product and examines how good writers go about this task.

The basic assumption behind the process view of writing is that students will slowly develop their thoughts and writing through a process of planning, drafting, revising, and editing (Seow, 2002). This means that the focus while writing is the process and not the final product. Writing as process involves writing several drafts and also considering the audience and purpose of the piece during this process. Writing as process means reflecting on one's own writing behaviors, a process which is aided by writing on topics of the writer's own interest. When writers reflect on their own writing behaviors, they begin to trust themselves as they write; they begin to view writing as a process of discovery of not only their thoughts, but also of who they are as writers.

Reflection Journal 3.6

First, write your own answers to these questions, and then find a partner or a group to discuss your findings and reflections; after these discussions in a pair or group, write a paragraph about your concluding reflections.

- In the previous sets of reflective questions, I asked about your thoughts on what you find the most difficult aspect of your writing. Read over your answer, and see if this can help you discover where along the continuum of writing, *product–process* you would place yourself in terms of your focus in writing.
- Some people say that they have a difficult time trying to find their "voice" when they are writing and this is especially true they say when they are writing in a second or foreign language. They say that they find the *product* approach to writing easier to follow because they can be guided more towards a definite end when they have been given an end model to emulate. They say that writing as a process does not make them feel when finished that they have accomplished a perfect piece of writing. What are you views on this idea of writer's "voice" vs. producing a composition from a model piece of writing?
- Can you identify your "voice" in your writing? Can you describe it?
- Why do you think that academic writing style sounds or reads as "stiff"?

My Own Process of Writing and Teaching Writing

In relation to the reflection questions posed above, I will share my views of how I write and teach writing, and you can decide what you think of them. For me, writing is a process of discovery in which writers not only discover what they are trying to say but also try to understand their own composing process. As I am in the process of discovering as I write, I know that most of my writing is not completed in one sitting. Many times, I get up and walk away, then come back later to work on the piece because I believe a writer needs distance and time away from writing for ideas to rest a while, germinate, and grow. Often, when I go jogging or out on an errand, whatever I am writing is never far from my mind. Sometimes, I even leave the piece I am working on for several weeks and then return to it with a fresh perspective.

When I was teaching English as a second language (ESL) writing, I built a process like my own into my classroom teaching of composition by having my students take breaks while writing their rough drafts and the multiple drafts that followed. We must remind our students that most writing does not begin at the beginning and proceed to the end (hence the earlier questions posed in the reflection journal). Writing is messy: writers get new ideas all the time, change their minds, and change direction in their writing. This is fine, and I (like most other writers) do this frequently and easily as I write. Sometimes, the beginning of a piece of writing for me is very different from the final product or what finally comes to print. Sometimes, I ask others to read what I have written although I know it is not finished. I do this because I want some more distance from it, and maybe I am also tired of it! I do not have to make the changes that are suggested by others because they may not know exactly what I am trying to say (of course, I may not know exactly what I am trying to say at that stage, either!), but I always find their comments refreshing and useful because they give me many new insights into my work that I did not have before I read their reflections.

Again, in my own teaching of ESL writing, I always had my students share their writing although they may not have always wanted to read their peers' work. So when they shared their writing, I gave them some specific questions that they had to answer rather than just doing a "free read" and making a general comment at the end. For example, I asked them to write what they perceived as the main points and the supporting details so the author could see if he or she had provided these clearly in the writing piece. However, I never asked them to check the grammar until the end because I find that this distracts students from the idea of writing content, context, and organization, which at an early stage is more important and relevant as a focus for writing. I do this in my own writing and check the grammar only at the end, just before I am ready to finish the whole process. I believe that most writing requires intervention of some sort by the author and/or by someone else (audience). Writing is collaborative and another person (a peer, friend, teacher, parents, etc.) can provide valuable input for the author as this input provides food for thought and reflection so that the writer can gain some perspective.

When I was teaching writing, I discovered that many second and foreign language students tend to be obsessed with the terror of making an error, to the extent that they can focus on little else. Consequently, on the first day of the writing class, in order to check students' anxiety levels concerning the nature of errors, I initiate a discussion about the inevitability of making errors in writing, and I show the class the errors I make in my own writing. This goes a long way to relaxing the students and motivating them to try to get their thoughts on paper regardless of making mistakes.

When I teach writing either to native English-speaking students or to students who use English as a second language, I always take the time to explain the writing process in detail to my students. I tell them how I write myself, show them examples of my writing process demonstrating that most writing goes through multiple rewrites and revisions. I show examples of my own writing as a process, along with examples from professional writers, and stress that multiple drafts are a fact of life for many of these professional writers. I get my students started with their writing by having as many whole-class instructional input sessions as feasible (i.e. given curricular and scheduling constraints) before they actually write.

These input sessions consist of *idea-generating activities* to help the students focus on the assignment. This type of process approach also recognizes that in some schools teachers may be obliged to give predetermined writing assignments – such as picture compositions and functional writing (e.g. how-to directions). However, even if the teacher chooses the type of assignment, it is also possible for each individual student himself or herself to decide the focus of the assignment, thus ensuring more responsibility and ownership of the piece of writing. Ideas for a topic to write about are generated by one or all of the following means:

- *Brainstorming*: Individuals, pairs, or groups generate (by speaking or writing) a number of possible topics and then write them on a piece of paper. Each individual, pair, or group reviews the list, and by a process of elimination of ideas the group consider not appropriate for the topic, arrives at a shortlist of topics to write about, through the final choice for a specific topic is left to each individual writer.
- *Freewriting*: After brainstorming, students can be encouraged to engage in a period of freewriting. Here the students are required to write as much as possible within a short period of time (usually 15 minutes), without focusing on correctness of grammar, sentence structure, or composition mechanics. Student pairs or groups can then read each other's work and suggest an alternative focus for the writing, other than grammar; in other words, grammar should not be a focus at this stage, only ideas.

Reflection Journal 3.7

First, write your own answers to these questions, and then find a partner or a group to discuss your findings and reflections; after these discussions in a pair or group, write a paragraph about your concluding reflections.

- What is your understanding of the phrase: "Writing is a process of discovery"?
- Research some famous or favorite writers to try to find out how they have written a piece in all its drafts before final publication. Of those writers, which do you think followed a product approach, which do you think followed a process approach, and how can you tell?
- After reading the sections on product and process, which approach did you follow in the past as you wrote, which do you think you will follow now, and why?
- Some people say that the process of writing is actually more satisfying than the product that is produced at the end of that process. Why do you think they would come to this conclusion?
- Do you agree that the process of writing is more satisfying than the product?

Ways to Write

Learning to Write

We learn to write by writing. Although this is a true statement, it does not really help you start the writing process itself because many of you probably find it difficult to write in the first place regardless of your education – or in some cases, *because* of your education. In fact, nobody ever showed me how to write, yet all my teachers expected me to be able to write well. When I made mistakes (as I did in every essay I wrote in grade school), teachers returned my papers with lots of red marks indicating the mistakes and their constant irritation that I continued to make such mistakes. I imagine that you might have had similar experiences. Yet many teachers never showed me why I was making the mistakes. In fact, because I never was explicitly taught how to write, I always had a difficult time getting my words on paper. As a result, when I entered graduate school, I was really worried about presenting my writing to my professors, to the point that I experienced writing anxiety each time I had to write. It was not until well into my graduate studies that I learned I did not have to put down my ideas perfectly the first time I put words on paper. I learned to write multiple drafts of my work and to follow steps in my writing. This next section outlines steps you can consider when writing. The steps I present are the same ones that I generally follow each time I write, but they can be adjusted by you depending on your reflective needs. I begin with getting words on paper (just write) and then show how to take it from there.

Reflection Journal 3.8

First, write your own answers to these questions, and then find a partner or a group to discuss your findings and reflections; after these discussions in a pair or group, write a paragraph about your concluding reflections.

- What are the ways you begin your writing?
- Do you ever have “writer’s block” (when you can’t write anything), and how do you solve this problem if you have it?
- Where are you most comfortable to begin writing?
- Where are you least comfortable to begin writing?
- Do you notice any habits or patterns in your ways of writing, either before you actually begin to put words down and/or when you begin to do so and just after this, as you really get into your writing process?

Getting Words on Paper

"Writer's block" is a phenomenon in which a writer just cannot get anything down on paper (or word processor), and it can become a real nightmare for someone who is writing for a deadline. Many times, however, I think it happens because the writer has lost faith in himself or herself and what he or she wants to write. I have found over the years that one of the best ways of physically getting words on paper is to *freewrite*. In freewriting, you just write whatever comes into your head and this process forces you to overcome the "block." The idea of the freewrite is not to produce a wonderful finished product of writing – far from it. In fact, many times this freewrite will produce nonsense at first. The writer has to learn to get back the trust in his or her abilities and to just keep going regardless of what is produced. As Elbow (1981: 14) maintains:

> Freewriting makes writing easier by helping you with the root psychological or existential difficulty in writing: finding words in your head and putting them down on a blank piece of paper. So much writing time and energy is spent *not* writing: wondering, worrying, crossing out, having second, third, and fourth thoughts.

In freewriting, you are engaged in the process of writing rather than the product, and as such, anything goes. Keep at it for 15 minutes or until you have completely exhausted whatever is inside your head. I have told many graduate students to just "puke" or spit out their thoughts on paper (disgusting, I know!). Leave blanks, misspell words, write half sentences, and keep moving and trying to keep up with your fast-moving thoughts. The most important thing for you is to get "it" out there on paper, whatever that "it" in your head is. Those of you who have been trained or who follow a product approach to writing may have to reconsider whether this approach is really helping you to write. I leave it up to you. Again, Elbow (1981: 15) points out that:

> Freewriting teaches you to write without thinking about writing. We can usually speak without thinking about speech – without thinking about how to form words in the mouth and pronounce them and the rules of syntax we unconsciously obey …

So freewriting in a sense emulates the freedom of spontaneous speech.

At this stage of my writing process, I do not worry about organization, grammar, or words, for that matter. I just let the whole thing – what I have written so far – fester (sorry for the sick metaphors, again). When I pick it up again, I start to consider why I am writing and who will eventually read it – that is, my audience – but I just keep them at the back of my mind at this stage. For me, stage one of writing is now over because something is on paper.

Reflection Journal 3.9

First, write your own answers to these questions, and then find a partner or a group to discuss your findings and reflections; after these discussions in a pair or group, write a paragraph about your concluding reflections.

- Do you think *freewriting* is useful?
- Have you ever done freewriting before?
- Try a freewrite on any topic of interest; write for 10 to 15 minutes without stopping: just try it and see what happens.
- What did you discover as a result of this freewrite?
- Was the process comfortable or not?

Revising

In the next stage of my writing, I begin to revise to make sense of what I have just written. When starting to revise, you must take care not to jump into a final product mode and remember that your revising will really not end until you give you written piece to your preferred audience to read. In my own case, I first think in terms of preparing a first draft during the revision period, the first of many such drafts as I refine what I have written. When revising, Elbow (1981: 38) suggests the following quick steps (in no particular order) to keep in mind:

- Try to keep outside yourself and get into a spirit of pragmatic detachment. Emphasize cutting.
- Keep your audience and purpose clearly in mind.
- Mark the good passages.
- Figure out the main point.
- Put the good passages in order. Perhaps make an outline.
- Add pieces that are missing.
- Write out a draft – excluding the beginning.
- Write the beginning; make sure you have a suitable conclusion.
- Tighten and clarify by cutting. Reading your draft out loud will help you experience it from a reader's point of view.
- Get rid of mistakes in grammar and usage.

At this stage, I take more careful notice of my intended audience and begin to shape the writing more with this audience in mind. This is also connected to the purpose of my writing: why am I doing this and who will read it? I first look at what points I have written and begin to put them in the order of importance that I want my readers to read. In other words, I begin to connect the dots of my writing that link my ideas: I look at how my paragraphs are structured and how the whole piece of writing is taking shape with these ideas and points in mind. I now join the paragraphs together and try to make a whole out of all the different pieces. I still do not worry too much about grammar or word choice at this stage. I am just trying to organize it all into one coherent piece of writing. I make sure I have made my statement of intent clear in my writing. Next, I begin to tackle my grammar mistakes and look for correct word usage and punctuation as I tighten up the whole piece. Elbow (1981: 38) suggests that now would be a good time to read your draft aloud so that you "experience it from a reader's point of view."

Reflection Journal 3.10

First, write your own answers to these questions, and then find a partner or a group to discuss your findings and reflections; after these discussions in a pair or group, write a paragraph about your concluding reflections.

- Do you follow any revision rituals?
- How many revisions are enough for you, and why?
- Are you ever satisfied with your finished written product? If not, why not?

Elbow (1981) summarizes all this nicely as he talks about the *loop process* of writing, which takes the writer on an elliptical orbiting voyage. As he suggests:

> For the first half, *the voyage out*, you do pieces of almost-free-writing during which you allow yourself to curve out into space – allow yourself, that is, to ignore or even forget exactly what your topic is. For the second half, *the voyage home*, you bend your efforts back into the gravitational field of your original topic as you select, organize, and revise parts of what you produced during the voyage out. (Elbow 1981: 60)

Writing as generally considered in an academic context is in the linear mode common in the English language, but there are many other types of writing that are possible when reflecting on your practice. Poetry is an example of a way you can write to express your reflections, and of course this has a long and esteemed tradition. I do not pretend to be able to write poems and cannot offer much in the way of my personal experiences with this genre as I don't have many poetry-writing experiences. Elbow (1981) suggests that we can all write poems if we follow a few simple rules. For example, he suggests that a good rule to start with is to write without too much thought a long string of lines without stopping, and begin each line with *I wish* because, he says: "It makes each sentence start itself with a bit of momentum so that more words just arrive without having to be sought" (Elbow, 1981: 102).

Reflection Journal 3.11

First, write your own answers to these questions, and then find a partner or a group to discuss your findings and reflections; after these discussions in a pair or group, write a paragraph about your concluding reflections.

- Elbow (1981: 61–73) suggests the following thirteen procedures for loop writing. What do you think of each, and do you follow any of these procedures as you write?
  1. *First thoughts*. Just put down as fast as you can all the thoughts and feelings you happen to have about the topic.
  2. *Prejudices*. What are you biases in the area of your topic?
  3. *Instant Version*. Turn out a kind of sketch of your final piece – an instant projected version.
  4. *Dialogues*. The main principle of dialogue writing is that you don't have to know ahead of time what a person is going to say. Just pick the speakers, get them talking, and see what they do say.
  5. *Narrative Thinking*. Write the *story of your thinking*.
  6. *Stories*. Start by letting stories and incidents come to mind and jotting them down very briefly.
  7. *Scenes*. Stop the flow of time and take still photographs. Focus on individual moments. What places, moments, sounds, or moods come to mind in connection?
  8. *Portraits*. Think about your topic and see what people come to mind. Give thumbnail portraits of them.
  9. *Vary the audience*. Write about your topic to someone very different from the real audience of your paper.
  10. *Vary the writer*. Write as though you were someone whose view on the topic is very different from you own. Or write as though you lived in a different culture.
  11. *Vary the time*. Write as though you were living in the past or the future.
  12. *Errors*. Write down things that are almost true or trying to be true, things that you are tempted to think or that others think but you know are false.
  13. *Lies*. Write down quickly all the odd or crazy things you can come up with.

Retrospective Writing

Retrospective writing is writing in which a writer reflects on a specific event that has occurred relatively recently. For example, teachers can write retrospective accounts about particular lessons they have just delivered and what they have experienced. An example of this is when I reported on a study in which teachers were asked to teach a lesson and then to write a retrospective account

Reflection Journal 3.12

First, write your own answers to these questions, and then find a partner or a group to discuss your findings and reflections; after these discussions in a pair or group, write a paragraph about your concluding reflections.

- Elbow (1981: 119) maintains that by "not making too big a deal of poetry – letting it be play-within-rules, letting it be about what it turns out to be about – you can write poems which please but don't try too hard. You will sometimes get a poem that is terrific or could be made so."
  - What do you think about this statement?
  - Try to write a poem using *I wish* ... at the start of each line, and don't stop for 10 minutes.
    I wish
    I wish
    I wish
  - Another one-line rule is to begin each line with *Once*. Now you try:
    Once
    Once
    Once
- Here are a few more ideas for writing poetry (original ideas from Elbow, 1981):
  - Write a short poem that begins with an action word.
  - Write a poem that begins with saying something nasty to someone.
  - Write a poem to a real person.
  - Write a group poem on any topic of interest.

Reflection Journal 3.13

First, write your own answers to these questions, and then find a partner or a group to discuss your findings and reflections; after these discussions in a pair or group, write a paragraph about your concluding reflections.

- Think about a particular lesson or class you are interested in reflecting on and write a retrospective account of that lesson or class immediately after teaching it, using the following questions as a guide (or change them as you wish):
  - What was your biggest concern as you were teaching this lesson/class, and why?
  - What influenced your instructional decisions most during this lesson/class, and why?
  - What have you learned from your answers to the above two questions?

in which they reflected on their experience (Farrell, 1999). Retrospective writing related to a particular lesson allows teachers themselves or other readers (including other teachers) to see how teachers make explicit their thinking in their post-lesson reflections. Teachers may use retrospective writing immediately after teaching particular lessons as a means of reflecting on their own work. Teachers can reflect on their biggest concern during the lesson and what influenced their instructional decisions most during that lesson, as a way to start a discussion with other teachers such as a critical friend or members of a writing group.

Chapter 3 Reflections

First, write your own answers to these questions, and then find a partner or a group to discuss your findings and reflections; after these discussions in a pair or group, write a paragraph about your concluding reflections after reading this chapter.

- Write a poem about your students.
- Write a poem about your colleagues.
- Write a poem about your teaching.
- Write a poem about you as a teacher.
- Write a poem about you that you think your students would write; then ask them to write a poem about you and compare the results.
- Complete the following sentences:
  - I like to write about my teaching because
  - I don't like to write about my teaching because
  - I like revising my writing because
  - I don't like revising my writing because
  - My favorite type of writing is
  - My least favorite type of writing is
  - Writing about my teaching helps me
  - Writing about my teaching is easier for me than
  - Writing my lesson plans helps me
  - Writing about my teaching beliefs helps me
  - Writing about my philosophy of teaching helps me
  - Writing about my teaching metaphors helps me
  - Writing about my teaching maxims helps me
  - Writing about my students helps me
  - Writing about my teaching context helps me
  - Writing about collaborations with my colleagues helps me
  - Writing about my use of textbooks helps me
  - Writing about my teaching methods helps me
  - Writing about my professional development helps me
  - Writing about my teaching doubts helps me
  - Writing about my teaching joys helps me
  - Writing about my observations of my class helps me
  - Writing about writing helps me

Conclusion

There are as many ways to write as there are writers. In this chapter, I have presented only a few and attempted to keep it simple, based on my own experiences as I write. For example, I have suggested that a general process approach (with modifications for context and the needs of both teacher and students) may a good means for second and foreign language teachers to use as they write and for their students to learn the skill of writing. In this approach, they are encouraged to reflect at every step of the writing process: from brainstorming, to initial outline, through each draft, and to the final draft. In this way, second and foreign language teachers and students can come to realize that writing is not just a finished product but also a process of discovering their own thoughts. In fact, I write this way myself – many drafts, many changes within each draft, and grammatical checking only at the end. The main reason I write is to see my own thoughts, so I can slow them down a bit, step back from them, and then reflect on where I am and where I want to go next.

4. The Reflective Teaching Journal

Preamble

I never wrote a diary or journal in my early life as I thought the whole idea was a complete waste of time, time I could not spend sitting at a desk again and doing what I hated to do in school, which was to write. It was not until I became a teacher that the idea of writing a diary/journal came up again and even so, I was still not so convinced of its use. This is what I was thinking at the time:

> We teachers are very busy and we do not have the time to spare to sit down and do something not fully related to our next day/week/month in class. If I have the time to sit down, I should use it to prepare my classes or mark those essays that have been sitting there for some time. What is the use of writing a journal or diary about my work? I spend enough time talking to other teachers about my job and the administration after work over coffee, and still we do not get an increase in pay or have better working conditions. I am so overwhelmed with work that if I have some spare moments, thinking about teaching would be the last thing that comes to my mind. In fact, I am probably close to burnout and rather than write about my teaching, I think I should take a nap.

Now I realize that this is the very reason many teachers are close to burnout: they do not take the time to reflect on what they are doing, how they are doing it, what the result is, or why they are doing what they are doing. They just keep going faster rather than slowing down for a moment or two to see where they are headed. And, yes, that was me, too, back all those years ago as I was teaching in Korea. I was speeding up my teaching rather than slowing it down – speeding up in reaction to those uneasy feelings that were beginning to rise within me that something needed to be changed and that I was not really sure about what I was doing in the classroom anymore. I know now that I did not know how to slow things down, even if I had wanted to do this, in order to reflect on my practice. But by chance one day, I started to write (with a pen) at home in a journal my wife gave me, and since I was writing for myself, I just wrote whatever came into my head at that time. Surprise, surprise – I actually enjoyed that moment and can still see where I was when I was writing that day.

Reflection Journal 4.1

First, write your own answers to these questions, and then find a partner or a group to discuss your findings and reflections; after these discussions in a pair or group, write a paragraph about your concluding reflections.

- Did you ever have a moment when you started to write about something and then found yourself writing nonstop for a long time without realizing the passage of that time?
- Did you read over your writing or do you not usually read over what you have written?
- What did you realize after you read over your own writing?
- Why do you think some people do not read over what they have written?
- What might be the benefit of reading over your own writing?
- Why do you think a person can write in a private journal for a long time but may be reluctant (or finds it difficult) to write for an audience such as colleagues the general public?

As mentioned in the previous chapter, reflection through writing enables people to step back and take stock of their thoughts because they can see them on paper or screen. For teachers, this process can be very helpful. As they begin to reflect on their practice, they can, as Richards (1990: 5) suggests, "move from a level where they may be guided largely by impulse, intuition, or routine, to a level where their actions are guided by reflection and critical thinking." A teaching journal is a place where a teacher writes regularly about his or her teaching experiences. Richards and Farrell (2005; 68) describe a teaching diary or journal as "an ongoing written account of observations, reflections, and other thoughts about teaching, usually in the form of a notebook, book, or electronic mode, which serves as a source of discussion, reflection, or evaluation." Bailey (1990) maintains that when language teachers write about various facets of their work over a period of time and then read over their entries looking for patterns, they may discover aspects of their teaching that they had not realized before writing the journal. Indeed, as I have said in previous chapters, when I started writing my own teaching journal over twenty years ago, I realized that I could not really say clearly what I thought until I had seen what I had written. The purpose of this chapter is to explore the impact of regular journal writing as a reflective tool for language teachers. The chapter outlines details about journal writing and offers suggestions, and some cautions, for language teachers, especially for language teachers who are not themselves native speakers of the language they are teaching, when using teaching journals to reflect on their work.

The Nature of Diaries/Journals

When we think of journals, we can cast our mind back to the time of the great travels of adventurers to all parts of the globe, from the cold of the poles to the heat of the jungles, many years ago. In their journals, those travelers wrote about their adventures; we eventually got to read them much later; and, depending on how they were written, we could get a good understanding of what they went through and what they saw and heard. Those journals were essentially not only a means by which the authors/adventurers could reflect on their immediate adventures, but also later a vehicle for others to reflect, to comment, and to learn from these experiences. Some called these diaries, logs, or calendars of events because they recorded events as they occurred at particular points in time, as in a ship's log or a spacecraft log (think *StarTrek*). Some authors wrote these for others to learn from, while other authors wrote them for their own learning; in other words, they wrote with the intention of informing their own knowledge and practices. These days, it is possible to record verbal journals for later reflection, such as in audio journals, or journals can be written so that others will write directly on these entries in a response to the entries, as in *dialogue journals* (e.g. Peyton and Reed, 1990). The point I want to make here is that journal writing has a long history; whether for adventure/travel writing or religious experience writing, this mode of reflection has been around for a long time. In the recent past, journal writing developed in the United States education system into a form of writing for learning that built on the work of Elbow (1981), as outlined in some detail in the previous chapter. The mantra that became popular then and has stayed in vogue to this day is this: *as we learn to write, we write to learn.*

For the purposes of this chapter, journal writing is seen as a means of not only recording what occurs but also of showing that the writer has an intentional reason to learn from the written records. Journal writers write down their thoughts and record what occurred around them so that they can return to this again, now that they have a record, in order to make more sense of these experiences and their thinking at that time and so that, as a result, they can learn from their experiences. Those who write a journal take responsibility and ownership for their own development because they are forced to stop and think not only as they write, but also as they try to make sense of their thoughts in their journals. They write to find something out that they did not know before starting to write (Richardson and St. Pierre, 1994; cited in Moon, 2006: 33). In other words, writing helps the writer to reflect in, on and for action.

Reflection Journal 4.2

First, write your own answers to these questions, and then find a partner or a group to discuss your findings and reflections; after these discussions in a pair or group, write a paragraph about your concluding reflections.

- Do you think journal writing can help with personal development?
- Do you think journal writing can help with professional development?
- Writing a journal is a way to record your experiences and then also to process these further as you read through your writing looking for patterns. What is your understanding of this statement?
- How does journal writing increase ownership of your experiences?
- How can journal writing help with your problem-solving?
- How can journal writing give voice to your experiences?
- Some authors have even stated that their journal is their personal friend. Why do you think this is the case?

Forms of Journal Writing

Journals can take many different forms, shapes, and sizes, and may not even have any physical form at all if in electronic, audio, or video format. That said, most journals have some sort of structure; otherwise, it would be difficult for journal writers to organize their thoughts in any coherent manner so they can make some sense of them. Usually, journal entries have a beginning and an end with dates noted of each entry to see where the thoughts originated. A person can write an autobiography to see and note various important events in life and how he or she progressed over time. Autobiographical writers try to note patterns in their development in order to learn more about themselves. They can then ask questions to themselves about these events. People can also come together to share their writing by, for example, asking questions to each other as in dialogue journals. In this way, the writers get another pair of eyes to help them see patterns that might be difficult for them to find by themselves. These days, technology has influenced much journal writing, with the development of blogs (or weblogs) on the Internet, but these are for public consumption and so issues of disclosure become important for the blog writer. Regardless what form a journal takes, writing can help you stop for a moment and get control of your thoughts so that you can stand back and try to make sense of these and learn more about yourself as a teacher and as a person, too.

Reflection Journal 4.3

First, write your own answers to these questions, and then find a partner or a group to discuss your findings and reflections; after these discussions in a pair or group, write a paragraph about your concluding reflections.

- From the discussion above, what form of journal writing would you be most comfortable with, and why?
- Which of the above types of teaching journal most appeals to you?
  - A notebook journal
  - A word-processed journal
  - A private journal
  - A blog journal
  - A journal with a critical friend
  - A collaborative electronic mail (e-mail) journal with a peer
  - A group journal (constructed as a group)
  - An audio-recorded journal
  - Other

Journal Writing and Reflection

When I was growing up, some of my friends kept a kind of journal of their thoughts; but I was never disciplined enough in those early years to stop for a while each day or each week to write about what was happening around me. It was not until I started travelling around the world later in my life that I started writing. At the time, so much was happening around me that I felt I needed some help to make sense of it all. I found that writing about events on paper helped me to gain some distance between myself and the event so that I could better understand it. Writing in a journal also made me slow down my thoughts enough to go beyond just noticing and to really consider what was happening. I slowly discovered that as I documented my travels and experiences, my own personal journey started to take shape: I began to notice certain patterns in my entries as they began to accumulate over months and years. In order to notice the patterns, it is necessary to read over the entries from time to time, and I found this process as important as the actual writing. Now I could learn from my experiences and indeed see some of the events that I thought were most serious at the time I wrote about them in a completely different light: they did not seem so serious when reflected on later in my journal. Journal writing allowed me to step back from events and in some instances led to new actions because of different interpretations I made while reading about them in print. Indeed, I was a reflective traveler at that time, and the practice I built up reflecting in that context eventually led me towards more easily becoming a reflective practitioner (although I did not know it at the time) in my life as a teacher.

Reflection Journal 4.4

First, write your own answers to these questions, and then find a partner or a group to discuss your findings and reflections; after these discussions in a pair or group, write a paragraph about your concluding reflections.

- Have you ever written any kind of diary or journal? If so, what kind of entries did you make?
- Have you ever written a travel journal or the like?
- Have you ever written a diary or journal about your learning of another language or any other type of learning? If so, what kind of entries did you make?

Teacher Journals

When I started my language teaching life in Korea in 1979, in a university language program in Seoul, I did not know what to expect as regards teaching and living in a new culture far away and far different from what I grew up with in Ireland. I did not know how to react to the students and how to "read" the students' faces in class, as they never showed much emotion in their faces or through their body language, as the culture is non-direct. (Later, I learned to read how Koreans react through their body language, but this took a long time.) A foreign teacher would not be told by the students if there were any problems occurring in class; the administration would tell the teacher. In order to try to make sense of my experiences during my first few months teaching in this completely new context, I started to write a teaching journal in which I would try to describe what occurred in my classes and what my reactions to it were. In this way, over the months I began to notice patterns in these events and in the way my students reacted, so that eventually the mystery of communication in a Korean classroom began to be revealed in my own journal writing. My Korean EFL teaching journal was my first real foray into reflective practice, although I was not familiar with this term at that time.

Journal writing can help language teachers question, explore, and analyze what they do both inside and outside the classroom. Reflective journal writing can give teachers time to think about their work for, as Holly (1989: 78) suggests, "long enough to reflect on it and to begin to understand and direct it." For example, teaching journals can act as a way to explore the origins and implications of a teacher's beliefs about language teaching and learning and as a way of documenting a teacher's classroom practices. Teachers can then compare their stated (written) beliefs with their recorded (as written in their teaching journals) classroom practices in order to monitor for any inconsistencies. Bailey (1990: 218) suggests that a teaching journal can be a place for teachers "to experiment, criticize, doubt, express frustration, and raise questions." McDonough (1994: 64–65) maintains that teachers who write regularly about their teaching can become more aware of "day-to-day behaviors and underlying attitudes, alongside outcomes and the decisions that all teachers need to take." Journals can also be a means for practicing teachers to reflect on problems that they encounter in classes as well as a way to see new teaching ideas so that they can better understand their own practice (Jarvis, 1996).

Bailey, Curtis, and Nunan (2001: 59) note four important reasons for keeping a teaching journal: to articulate problems in teaching, to vent frustrations, to clarify certain issues, and to stretch oneself professionally. They say that by articulating problems and venting frustrations about teaching, teachers can come to clearer realizations about their teaching, and that all this leads to professional development. I would like to add to their four reasons a fifth, and it is that teaching journals may be used to write about and to celebrate successes in teaching.

Reflection Journal 4.5

First, write your own answers to these questions, and then find a partner or a group to discuss your findings and reflections; after these discussions in a pair or group, write a paragraph about your concluding reflections.

- Have you ever written a teaching journal (exclusively about teaching)? If so, what kind of entries did you make?
- If you have never written any kind of diary or journal, do you think it would be useful for a language teacher (or student) do write a journal? If yes, what kind of entries would you expect to find in such a journal?
- Now would be a good time to begin your teaching journal. In order to start, you will consider the following questions first:
  - Will you use a computer or an ordinary notebook?
  - Will you organize your writing or will you just freewrite your thoughts (and maybe organize these later)?
  - Who is your audience: yourself, a peer, or an instructor (e.g. in a graduate course)?
  - What will you focus your writing on: a lesson, a technique/method, a theory, a question posed, or some aspect of your job outside the classroom?
  - How regularly will you write: after a lesson, daily or once a week?
  - How regularly will you review what you have written: every two or three weeks? More often? Less often?

Case Study of Teaching Journal: "Seeing My Thoughts"

Background

I now use a case study of the journal writings of teachers within the teacher development group in Korea which I facilitated (Farrell, 1996). I use this case study as an illustration of what teachers write about in journals concerning their teaching, how reflective they can become when writing, and my reflections on what they were writing about.

Procedures

Initially, all three teachers agreed that each participant would keep an ongoing journal account of their experiences during the period of their group's existence. They agreed at the beginning that they could write about anything, whenever they wanted, but they also agreed to write at least one entry after any classroom event that was unusual or interesting. The teachers gave me access to all of their journal entries.

Journal Topics

Generally, the most frequent topic all three teachers wrote about in their journals focused on their *approaches and methods of teaching*, followed by *evaluating their teaching*, and then by their *theories of teaching*. I now outline what each teacher's individual journal entries showed.

Teacher 1

Teacher 1 (T1), out of a total of 22 entries, was most concerned with evaluating her teaching rather than any other aspect of her work. She frequently cited problems, both personal and teaching-related, as influencing her teaching. For instance, she wrote in her journal about some personal problems she was facing while she was teaching: "I have not been feeling well these days and today I have a weak fever and dizziness. That means I did not fully prepare for the class. That made me a little upset." Later on during the semester, this bad feeling would get worse: "October is a cruel month. I have lost appetite for teaching" and "Today I hardly could concentrate on the class. These days everything went wrong. I have too many things to handle right now. I experienced blackout in my mind … I felt as if I were a basket case"

T1 also reflected on the events that gave rise to difficulties in her teaching and tried to generate her own solutions. One such difficulty she had concerned the issue of how and when to correct her students' language errors. In an early journal entry, she addressed this issue when she was considering how to correct students in a pronunciation class:

> One of my weakest points is voiced sounds like [z] in zoo or museum. But I'm not an English native speaker, too. My English

> is not perfect. I always feel sorry about that to my students. Nevertheless, I try to correct their pronunciation but the result is not good. I know it takes some time and requires a lot of practice. Besides, I'm afraid my too often correction will make them silent and cause negative effect. So I refrain from correction too often. This is my dilemma.

A later entry notes that while T1 had not solved her dilemma, she had become more comfortable with it. She was teaching a speech class in which one student would lead the class in a discussion of a topic. She wrote about her method of correction:

> In fact, I meant to comment on his grammatical problems but I changed my mind. Because I, as teacher, made many mistakes, too. I felt whenever I opened my mouth I was making a mistake. Nevertheless our communication worked. Isn't that our aim to learn a language? Besides, I don't want to dampen cold water on his enthusiasm to practice English.

T1 also wrote a lot about her teaching procedures, which suggested that her experience was mostly from the classroom and previous experiences as a student. This seems to be consistent with statements from her autobiographical interview, in which she mentioned that she had no TESOL qualifications and only entered EFL teaching at her professor's strong suggestion.

Teacher 2

Teacher 2 (T2), the native-speaking teacher and the most prolific of the three writers, with 28 entries, sharply contrasted with T1, who had fewer and shorter entries. An example from T2's journal addresses the topic of how he as a teacher made decisions in class:

> We must extend the wait time before we make a decision as long as we can stand the uncertainty, as we extend it waiting for a student response. The teacher as passive? I'm not talking here about action. When we know what to do, we should do it straight away. But when we don't know what to do, we should wait and savor the uncertainty. This is what makes teaching a buzz anyway, the uncertainty.

T2 also wondered about the place of training for language teachers, in that he saw little place for special training of teachers in language instruction. He wrote:

> The classroom is not the best place to learn a language because the teachers cop out as a result of the emotional demands and the intellectual demands placed on them. Learning from a partner in a familiar relationship who is prepared to talk about, answer questions about language is better. This partner does not require any special training. Special training cannot really help this person teach better. But in the classroom the intellectual and emotional stress can prevent the teacher acting as a partner would.

As these comments illustrate, T2 was mainly concerned about his decision-making in the classroom as well as how a person can be best trained as a teacher.

Teacher 3

Teacher 3 (T3) was the least active in her journal writing, with only six entries. In fact, throughout the whole reflective process (12 weeks), T3 was somewhat ambivalent about exploring her teaching. For example, in her first journal entry she wrote:

> What do I think about my teaching method? Do the students learn something from my teaching? I don't want to answer these questions. Actually I don't know.

In her next journal entry one month later, she wrote that she might not be happy using journal writing as a means of reflecting on her teaching. She further remarked:

> I'm happy when we (our group) talk about our classes, even though I am sometimes wondering whether I'm heading for the right direction to find myself as a teacher. I'm also afraid of knowing myself in some ways.

It is quite possible that writing in English may have been a burden for her, and as such, maybe it would have been better if she had written in her native language, Korean. Additionally, she could have audio-recorded her entries if English and time were her main problems. Although she never stated that English was problematic for her writing, T3 did mention in one group meeting that it was time-consuming to sit and think about what to write.

These three teachers had the courage to reflect on their own teaching and also had the courage to share their reflections with each other in a group and with a group facilitator. What is interesting is that such group reflective

Reflection Journal 4.6

First, write your own answers to these questions, and then find a partner or a group to discuss your findings and reflections; after these discussions in a pair or group, write a paragraph about your concluding reflections.

- Consider the topics covered by the teachers T1, T2, and T3, and comment about what you noticed or what struck you about their reflections.
- The most frequent topic the teachers wrote about in their journals focused on their *approaches and methods to teaching*, followed by *evaluating their teaching* and then their *theories of teaching*. What do you think about these topics, and are they important for you?
- The experienced teachers in the study I conducted wrote about the following topics (in order):
  1. Approaches and methods of teaching
  2. Evaluating teaching
  3. Theories of teaching
  4. Self-awareness of oneself as a teacher
  5. Questions about teaching
- Which of the 5 topics above would you write about in a teaching journal? Why?
- Try to think of other topics you might write about in teaching.
- Look at the individual entries each teacher made and comment on them.

practice was not popular at that time in that context (South Korea) and as such was a major innovation within English as a foreign language teacher development initiatives. Of course, each teacher reflected on different concerns associated with his/her work, but the group as a whole attempted to comment on these issues even if many remained unresolved. The main highlight of the group discussions was the emotional support these provided for each of the members and the further realization that teaching is such an isolated act that emotional support is very important for all teachers.

Facilitator Reflections

Although Ho and Richards (1993), in a survey of 32 teachers' evaluations of their experiences of writing a teaching journal, discovered that most of the teachers found that practice useful or at least fairly useful, they also discovered that some did not enjoy writing a journal. In the Ho and Richards (1993) study, the most common reasons for not wanting to write a teaching journal were that: (1) it is time-consuming; (2) it can become tedious after some time; and more importantly, (3) some teachers really do not enjoy writing a journal or diary as a form of reflection. It is this latter point that I was interested in pursuing with regard to the findings of the case study outlined in this chapter that indicated T3 did not enjoy writing a teaching journal. So I revisited the transcripts of the group meetings, and any transcribed individual meetings I had with T3, to look for instances when T3 commented on her reflections and on writing a teaching journal.

Two striking and related patterns emerged from my revisit to the transcripts: the first was T3's reluctance (and fear) to reflect in general, and the second was her fear about using teaching journals as a means of reflection. Regarding her reluctance and unease with reflection, this was present as early as the second group meeting (September 10), when T3 commented about having to reveal details about her classes to the other participants in the group. T3 stated: "Nobody can get into my class. I know what is going on, so I and we can check ourselves." Also, in a discussion I had with T3 when we were just getting the details of the reflective cycle for the group under way (Week 3 of the reflective process), she said that she was very uncomfortable "thinking" about her teaching. She said, "I hate looking at myself while I'm teaching." Later, in a group meeting when the other participants were exchanging information and views about what they were doing in their classes and sharing their teaching journals (usually orally at the start of each meeting, although sometimes participants exchanged their written journals), T3 said that she was not comfortable talking about her teaching and, in fact, did not bring her teaching journal to the group meetings from that point onwards. She commented:

> I know one way of teaching. I want to talk about teaching in the group but I think that [talking about our teaching] together in a group and talking about specific aspects of teaching are dangerous because the group can be judgmental.

After this meeting, and at most of the group meetings from then on, T3 rarely commented on her teaching techniques or methods, focusing almost exclusively on her teaching context and the problems associated with this context. From my perspective as a critical friend, it seems that T3 had exhibited a pattern of avoidance to reflect on teaching early on in the reflective process, and this was exacerbated by a requirement (made by the group in the first meeting) that she would have to write a journal about her reflections that would be read by other group participants. Thus, for T3, having to write a journal may have heightened the already increasing levels of unease she was experiencing about her work. For example, she said she stopped writing in her journal after a few weeks because she did not want the other participants to judge her teaching. She reflected:

> I don't want to go inside of that specific matter [writing about my teaching in detail]…. I mean everybody got a different point of

> view, so how can I judge other peoples' opinion. We have a different point of view...about teaching, we disagree with each other, right?

Additionally, at the last group meeting, T3 said that for her, writing a teaching journal was "cruel" because "this gave me stress, I always had to write something down, but I didn't have anything to write." Having to write in a second language may also have been a contributing factor to increasing T3's stress levels of writing and reflecting, although she did not mention this to me or others in the group.

So while writing a teaching journal may facilitate the reflective process for the majority of language teachers and so relieve some of the stresses of teaching, for some teachers (a minority), writing a reflective journal may lead to increased levels of anxiety that may be associated with reflecting in general and with the act of writing itself. For example, in the case study reported in this chapter, writing a teaching journal required that all three teachers spend a lot of time on this type of self-analysis. One can also speculate that for the two non-English speaking native teachers (T1 and T3), who had to write in a second language, this writing process took more time than it would for native speakers. These two teachers not only had to write reflectively about their teaching and to deliberate over what they had written; they also had to consider their word choice, grammar, and organization. This may have added enough of an extra burden to undercut the value of reflecting in the first place. Yet even for many language teachers writing in a second or foreign language, journal writing enhances their level of awareness about their teaching and

Reflection Journal 4.7

First, write your own answers to these questions, and then find a partner or a group to discuss your findings and reflections; after these discussions in a pair or group, write a paragraph about your concluding reflections.

- Why do you think some teachers find it difficult to write about their teaching in any meaningful way?
- What do you think about T3's comment that writing a teaching journal was "cruel" because "this gave me stress, I always had to write something down, but I didn't have anything to write."
- According to Burton (2005: 14), there are several reasons why teachers don't write about teaching:
  - Lack of time
  - Lack of support to write
  - Lack of confidence in their abilities to write
  - Lack of reward or recognition as teachers when they do write.

  Address each of these points and say which you think is the most important reason, and why. Can you add any more reasons?

about how their students learn, potentially enriching their lives as teachers. Nonetheless, as this case study shows, reflection is not always an easy process and may take some adjustment and time to get used to.

Using Teaching Journals Effectively

This section outlines how teachers can overcome some of the difficulties of writing about their teaching as outlined in the research above and in the last question posed above. Beginning to write is probably the most difficult of all aspects of reflective writing for teachers. It is always difficult to start writing a teaching journal because there are so many topics that language teachers can choose to focus on, from micro-level topics such as *group work in class*, *giving of instructions*, *the use of questions*, and *giving feedback/correction of errors*, to more macro-level concerns such as *lesson planning*, *textbook selection*, *curriculum development*, and *administration influences*. Both micro- and macro-level lists of issues that concern teachers are virtually endless. With that in mind, I suggest that teachers start reflecting through journal writing by beginning with a general topic, rather than jumping into their own teaching with too critical or broad a view. I have found over the years that language teachers can be their own worst critics, focusing for the most part only on the negative and completely forgetting to note what they do well and what is successful in their classrooms. Teachers can decide if they want to write their journal by word processing or with a pen on paper, or if they want to record their journal entry verbally with an audio-recording device. After some time, teachers can look for any patterns they see emerge in the entries and then focus on a specific finding for a period of time, possibly by engaging in an action research project that critically explores whatever theme or pattern has emerged.

Alternatively, teachers who already have issues which they consider important to them can explore these issues by writing about them in their journals. However, sometimes teachers' important issues may remain at a subconscious level of reflection as the teacher broods on something without realizing it. I have found that attempting to answer the following question is useful in raising those subconscious reflections to the level of conscious awareness: *Reflect on a recent teaching practice or experience in the classroom, positive or negative, that caused you to stop and think about your teaching.* In attempting to answer such a question, language teachers will reflect (through journal writing) on their assumptions and beliefs about the experience they have recalled, thus beginning the process of becoming more critical reflective practitioners. Additionally, I suggest that teachers continue to write about the focused topic for at least a month while reviewing their entries each week. At the end of the month, it may be a good idea to write a summary of some of the important events that arose, such as some classroom or career critical incidents, and what has been learned as a result of the reflection process.

Additionally, teachers should consider whether they want to share their journals with other teachers or keep their reflections private. Richards and Farrell (2005) suggest that teachers should decide on who their audience will be, as this may change the way they write and the amount they are willing to reveal. If teachers have written a journal to share with their peers, they should decide on what text they want their peer(s) to read; teachers can block text by stapling pages together that they do not want made public, or they can write a different version (a summary, perhaps) for others to read. For example, in the case study outlined in this chapter, T3 could have omitted the entries she did

Reflection Journal 4.8

First, write your own answers to these questions, and then find a partner or a group to discuss your findings and reflections; after these discussions in a pair or group, write a paragraph about your concluding reflections.

- This activity will attempt to focus your writing. Try to write a journal entry for yourself, a peer/critical friend, or a group that includes the following steps:
  - Focus on a recent issue you found important in your teaching or an actual problem you encountered in your teaching.
  - Now, try to analyze that problem in light of your beliefs about teaching and learning.
  - Next, attempt some interpretations of what you have found. If you are writing for a critical friend or a group, ask the person or group for feedback on the analysis and interpretation.
  - Last, ask yourself what all this means to you as a teacher. Do you need to change anything?
- Do you think the format (above) for formal journal writing is helpful or not? Explain.
- Here are some questions that a teacher can attempt to answer in his or her journal as a means of reflecting on teaching practice from a general point of view. Rather than focusing on a particular problem or issue, here a teacher looks at his or her teaching from a broad perspective. Teachers may want to use feedback from classroom observations to help them answer these questions. When the teacher has written answers to these questions, he or she can share with another teacher or a group of teachers in order to get some more feedback.
  - Describe what you do in a descriptive way, with no judgment.
  - Why do you do what you do?
  - How does what you do compare to what other teachers do?
  - What is the result?
  - Should you continue to do this or change it?
  - What change will you make?

not want the other participants to read, thus continuing her writing, rather than stopping altogether in fear of revealing her reflections.

One further important issue associated with journal writing that teachers should be aware of is that starting a teaching journal may not be enough for critical reflection, as there is a real danger that journal writing can fizzle out as the teacher becomes less willing to write if there is no real purpose to the writing. Language teachers should engage in *systematic reflection* when using teaching journals as a reflective tool. For example, Richard and Farrell (2005) suggest that teachers should first set attainable goals for their writing, the most important one being why they want to write the teaching journal. For example, are you going to focus on a specific problem in your teaching, or are you going to write with a general focus and look for patterns in your teaching over time, such as every month? Additionally, teachers should make sure they have enough time to do journal writing and decide when to write the journal and the number of entries to write. Richards and Farrell (2005) also suggest that teachers review their journal content regularly in order to learn from it and to consider whether they have achieved what they had intended when they started their journal writing.

Conclusion

The idea of reflection encompassed in this chapter goes beyond the fleeting thought after class. Rather, reflection is seen as a learned activity in which writing can facilitate the reflection process; teachers can write about their

Chapter 4 Reflections

First, write your own answers to these questions, and then find a partner or a group to discuss your findings and reflections; after these discussions in a pair or group, write a paragraph about your concluding reflections after reading this chapter.

- How is journal writing a means of telling your story?
- How can you "reread yourself" by reading through journal entries?
- How can journal writing help you develop your awareness?
- How can journal writing not only explore your experiences but also widen them?
- How can journal writing help you develop your creativity?
- Some say journal writing can initiate changes in a person's life. How do you think this would be possible?
- The most stated problem with writing a journal is the issue of time. How can you overcome this issue to make sure you write regularly?
- Another issue with writing a journal that others are going to read is self-disclosure. How can you deal with this issue?

teaching practices and then review and reflect on observed patterns that may emerge from their writing. It is the very process of writing that helps teachers to consciously explore and analyze their practice. As the results of the case study presented in this chapter suggest, writing may not be suitable as a means of reflection for all teachers, for different reasons, such as fear of revealing one's reflections in writing or difficulty with the writing process itself. Nonetheless, for the majority of language teachers, writing seems to be an efficient means of facilitating reflection, and it has an added advantage in that it can be done alone or be shared with other teachers. If teachers share their reflections, they can attain different perspectives about their work from the reflections of others.

5. Narrative Reflective Writing

Preamble

We all have a story to tell, and the old adage that everyone has 15 minutes of fame is actually quite true as it relates to a person's story: the story of one's life. Teachers too have a story or, in fact, many stories, related to their experiences both inside and outside the classroom. Considering the total number of students that one teacher will encounter in his or her teaching career, one can imagine the number of stories that each teacher will have. I remember my first story from my teaching career. I was in my teaching practice school in Dublin, Ireland, where I delivered lessons for two hours each morning as part of my teacher education course at university. One particular morning, I was teaching a class of junior high school students when suddenly one student blurted out, after I had given them their homework assignment for the following class, "Teacher, you are stupid!" As a novice teacher learning my profession, I can say that I was shocked to hear this from a young teenager, who said it loudly to my face. I remember telling him that this was not appropriate language to use to me or anyone else in class, that he must write a letter of apology to me that night, and that when I read it, I would consider letting him back to class the following day or else send him to the principal.

He wrote the letter and in it he said: "Teacher, I called you stupid because you were stupid because you gave us the same homework the day before and that is why you are stupid." The letter continued on to say he was sorry. (I think his parents made him put this in!) In some ways he was correct, as I realize that I made a mistake with the homework assignment for that class and possibly also I was in fact a bit "stupid." Nevertheless, I told him not to use that particular language again during class. I still have the student's letter today, by the way. I learned from this experience that students are not "stupid" and that teachers had better prepare well and make sure they are keeping up with their own lessons. I also learned that students do listen to you, even though they may seem to be texting or doing other things besides paying attention. I believe that young people can multi-task doing many different things, although it may seem that they are not giving you their full attention. This short narrative is a reminder that students have a voice and also a right to talk and respond to what we teachers assign them.

Reflection Journal 5.1

First, write your own answers to these questions, and then find a partner or a group to discuss your findings and reflections; after these discussions in a pair or group, write a paragraph about your concluding reflections.

- Do you have any short story from your early teaching days, either during teaching practice (such as my narrative above) or during your first year(s) of teaching, that can be instructive to you as a teacher today?
- What is your first memory as a student?
- Why do you think you still remember this?
- What is your first memory as a teacher or student-teacher?
- Why do you think you still remember this?

Telling our story to ourselves and others can be instructional because we are able to learn more about ourselves as we reflect on the meaning of our stories to explain who we are and who we want to become. So too can narrative reflection focused on classroom experience be useful for teachers, regardless of their experience levels, because they can learn about their own professional identities as they look for meaning from their professional journeys. Narrative reflective practice is valuable for language teachers because they can obtain new understandings of themselves when they reflect on their own perspectives of teaching and learning. These self-reflection stories can provide a rich source of teacher-generated information that allows teacher-writers to reflect on how they got where they are today; how they conduct practice; the thinking and problem-solving they employ during their practice; and their underlying assumptions, values, and beliefs that have ruled their past and current

Reflection Journal 5.2

First, write your own answers to these questions, and then find a partner or a group to discuss your findings and reflections; after these discussions in a pair or group, write a paragraph about your concluding reflections.

- How can telling their professional story help teachers reflect?
- What is your understanding of the term *narrative*?
- In what way would writing your teaching stories be different than telling your teaching stories?
- Which form of reflection (writing or telling) would be most useful to you, and why?

practices. This chapter outlines how language teachers can gain self-awareness by writing their stories, thus taking the first step in gaining insight into and control over what they are experiencing as teachers: the frustrations, problems, or isolating experiences of life in the classroom as well as the opportunities, the joy, and the sense of connection with students. By writing their stories, language teachers can begin to adopt strategies in which they can deal with some of the problems they may encounter throughout their careers as teachers. This chapter offers language teachers ways in which they can analyze their own written narratives, critical incidents, and case studies so that they can see more clearly their roles and careers in teaching.

Narratives and Reflection

Storytelling, in the form of narrative, had been a main means of transferring information from one generation to the next until writing was invented. Indeed, as Connelly and Clandinin (1990: 2) have noted, "Humans are storytelling organisms who, individually and collectively, lead storied lives." Thus, narratives illustrate our view of the world. As Garro and Mattingly (2000: 1) suggest, "in both telling and interpreting experiences, narrative mediates between an inner world of thought-feeling and an outer world of observable actions and states of affairs." By telling and retelling our stories, we can begin to reconceptualize our own history so that we can move to a place that we control rather than a place that we have been unwittingly placed.

We all have a story to tell because we have all lived and accumulated many different kinds of experiences. Miccoli (2008: 66) defines experience as "a process of relationships and emotional dynamics that temporarily involves experience, experienced and context of experience." These experiences are revealed in our storytelling, and by reflecting on them we can engage in self-inquiry. As Connelly and Clandinin (1990: 2) maintain, "the study of narratives is the study of the ways humans experience the world" Therefore, through narrative inquiry, we can reflect on the impact of our experiences and what they mean in terms of our assumptions, beliefs, and actions. According to Johnson and Golombek (2002: 4):

> [I]nquiry into experience that is educative propels us to not only question the immediate context but to draw connections among experiences – what Dewey calls *continuity of experience* (1933), or how experiences change the conditions under which new experiences are understood so that a person's abilities, desires, and attitudes are changed. Inquiry into experience, in this sense, can be educative if it enables us to reflect on our actions and then act with foresight.

Reflection Journal 5.3

First, write your own answers to these questions, and then find a partner or a group to discuss your findings and reflections; after these discussions in a pair or group, write a paragraph about your concluding reflections.

- This journal is about knowing the self through autobiography and follows Stanley's (1992: 158) suggestion that the concepts "biography and autobiography are inseparable dimensions of the same experience." In other words, talking (or writing) about your life means you actively (re)construct that knowledge using your own life story – your individual history, or biography – to reflect on who you are as a teacher, thus creating a personal view of that biography: in essence, your own *teacher's autobiography*. Narratives can be long chronological stories about where we came from, or they can be narrations of shorter critical incidents in our lives that have deeply affected us in some way. I will deal with critical incidents later in this chapter. For now, begin writing your autobiography and include pertinent references to any critical incidents within your story. For this reflection, include the following:
  - When and where you were born
  - Your early years
  - Your early school years
  - Your high school years
  - Your college years
  - Your decision to become a language teacher
  - Your first teaching experience

Teacher Narratives

Teachers can use narratives, as mentioned earlier, to reflect on their practice by writing their stories because these stories reveal the "knowledge, ideas, perspectives, understandings, and experiences that guide their work" (Johnson and Golombek, 2002: 7). According to Johnson and Golombek (2002: 6), teacher narratives tell the "stories of teachers' professional development within their own professional worlds." Language teachers can get insight from the stories they construct because these stories express their identities, their personal experiences, and even the conflicting beliefs and values that they have accumulated throughout their teaching lives. By writing their stories, teachers can gain a clearer picture about many things, such as:

- What it is they actually do both inside and outside the classroom in relation to their work (such as in the staff room, interacting with students and parents outside the classroom, and in other contexts);
- Who they are as professionals;

- What their beliefs, assumptions, values, theories, and practices are, and where these have come from;
- Who they teach, their students' identities and needs; and
- The context in which they are teaching.

Teachers have their own beliefs about their practices and their own assumptions about language education; yet most of these are hidden from the very people who should know: the teachers themselves. Narrative telling or writing can bring these usually tacitly held beliefs to the level of conscious awareness. Then teachers can decide which of their beliefs and practice remain relevant at a particular point in their lives and careers, with the ultimate aim of self-renewal.

Thus, by telling or writing their stories, teachers can feel cathartic relief, as the story-telling process offers an outlet for tensions, feelings, and frustrations about teaching (Jalongo and Isenberg, 1995). I would suggest that writing your teaching stories is more beneficial than telling your stories because there is a place to pause when you write that can aid your thinking about what it is you are trying to tell. Writing your teaching stories disciplines you as the teller in a way that telling your teaching stories may not be able to, as you blurt out whatever comes to your mind at that time and you rush to get everything out through the medium of speech without any real organization of what comes out. Of course, you can record these stories and reflect on the spoken word later and then write what it is you think is important from the spoken work. Even so, writing may offer teacher-writers a kind of disciplining they may need as they consider specific episodes in their professional lives. For example, according to Jalongo and Isenberg (1995: 162), writing their story can offer teachers "a safe and nonjudgmental support system for sharing the emotional stresses and isolating experiences of the classroom." For teacher education programs, McCabe (2002) suggests that stories can set off a dialogue about teaching that can offer strategies for dealing with problems first-year teachers may face as well as the successes they manage.

Dutra and Mello (2008) maintain that when teachers self-observe in their teaching narratives, they can reconceptualize their practice. In other words, teachers are able to reflect on their own narratives to discover their underlying assumptions, values, and beliefs about teaching and learning in order to become more aware of who they are as teachers. In other words, for teachers, narratives are a useful reflective tool because this story-telling allows teachers to gain not only a deep understanding of their professional selves, but also of the impact of their experiences on their current teaching practices. As a consequence, teachers may be able to challenge their deeply hidden assumptions and to make changes to those assumptions which they find are no longer relevant to their current professional outlook.

Reflection Journal 5.4

First, write your own answers to these questions, and then find a partner or a group to discuss your findings and reflections; after these discussions in a pair or group, write a paragraph about your concluding reflections.

- The following is a narrative written by an experienced ESL college teacher in Canada (adapted from Farrell, 2007). Read the story and write answers to the reflective questions that follow.

I was teaching a course entitled Socio-cultural Influences on Teaching English as a Second Language. It was in the autumn term, 3 hours per week; most of the students were university graduates who wanted to become ESL/EFL teachers. Students were required to complete a survey called the Key Performance Indicators (KPI) that is done across the province by all colleges. It is the primary source of information about the course, and we are held accountable for the responses. For example, in previous years, there was a very low evaluation in our KPIs related to college facilities, so that we, as a department, had to hold a focus group with our students to better understand their responses. We discussed the low ratings with our program advisory committee, and the program chair had to come up with strategies for improvement.

The survey asks students to comment on a very wide range of things, from the actual learning experience and program quality to college resources, facilities, technology, cafeteria/bookstore, skills for future career, right down to teacher punctuality. Students complete it at the end of the program. Not all courses in a program have to complete the survey every term, and not all programs necessarily do one every year. Because it is so extensive, they take a cross-section of programs in the college (I think). It is the type of survey where a statement is given and the students can mark their answer on a continuum: *agree strongly*, *agree*, *neither agree nor disagree*, *disagree*, disagree strongly (something like that).

The student in this incident was one who had repeatedly, from the very first class, demonstrated a contemptuous boredom with the program as a whole. He had indicated this in a number of ways to all his teachers. In person, he was tactfully polite, but in his written assignments, he would express his truer feelings. He always seemed to resist or think he was above what we were teaching in the program. We suspected that his fiancée, who was also in the program, had dragged him there so that they could travel overseas together. He had just completed university and seemed to think he was above a college program – although this is now my own perception, as I seek to understand why someone would stay in a program that he clearly didn't like. Because the negative feedback came from this student, I could have dismissed it more easily. It was predictable; of course, he didn't like anything. It was really not a surprise. And yet, I still felt the sting of the negative result and comments and had to reflect upon why. Then we did our official surveys and I could tell from, you know, how they give you the bar graph or the percentages showing, you know, *disagree*, *neutral*, and then *agree*. Seven percent were always that *disagree*, which indicates out of a class of whatever it was, 19 or whatever, that one person HATED everything.

- Can you identify the following parts of the story:
  - Who is the story about?
  - When did the story take place?
  - Where did the story take place?
  - What happened?
- Can you identify the problem this teacher encountered?
- Can you identify a turning point in the story?
- Can you outline a possible resolution to this problem?
- What do you think this reflection means for the teacher in the story?
- Now read how the teacher evaluated her incident and her idea of the final result, and then write your responses to the teacher's evaluation and result below (adapted from Farrell, 2007).

I was very disturbed by some unsolicited comments from a TESL (Teaching English as a Second Language) student at the end of December. Even after all our talk about feedback from students and our ability to take feedback and make changes, and not taking it personally. I was amazed by my hugely negative, emotional response. Just when you think you're above the fray, bam, some negative feedback hits you between the eyes. After doing some thinking on the experience, I have come to realize that it wasn't the comment itself that disturbed me (basically, because I knew it was not valid), but the fact that this student felt he had a right to criticize the course content (and indirectly, me) despite the fact that he had not attended a significant portion of the course and actually failed the final exam. The fact is that I felt vulnerable. I think I was worried that someone (Other teachers?? Not sure) was going to listen to this guy and that judgments would be made about this course and about me. I'm totally over that. In fact, I think I am probably a more severe critic of myself than anyone else could be. I wasn't concerned by the positives or the negatives or the neutrals. I mean, I looked at them, and it was interesting and there were not really surprising things; but I knew that that was him and it was like, oh well. So I feel empowered by our PD [professional development workshop]. I don't know if it's a direct result of our PD. The surveys never actually give you anything really, really concrete to do in your class but you get this feedback and then you're like, well what do I… What do I do with this? How does it affect me? Now, it's different. So, I think by openly discussing the surveys…. Then today, today I had to send out the "Have Your Say," like our ESL teachers do a mid-term survey called Have Your Say. Basically, the way it's structured is the different skills thumbs-up / thumbs-down.

- What is your reaction to the teacher's response above?

Writing a Narrative

There are many different ways to write a narrative about what you do. You can freewrite without paying attention to the organization, grammar, or word choice, as discussed previously. You can, alternatively, write a poem that tells your story, or you can write your story in a formal essay style that is structured into paragraphs and follows formal writing conventions. Any of these ways of writing will be useful for teachers, and many will have other different ways to write that will make perfect sense to them. However, when you write a narrative, you should do so with the idea of making sense of it or analyzing what you write; and in order to do this, you must follow some framework to make it workable and useful so you can reach the level of awareness that you are seeking. In using a particular framework as you write, you are actually also making your next job, the analysis, much easier and clearer than if you had to spend a lot of time going through all your bits and pieces of unstructured writings. When writing a narrative, I use an adapted version of Cortazzi's (1994: 159) framework for narratives for both my writing and later as a framework for analyzing; the framework uses four main phases in writing and analysis: *orientation*, *complication*, *evaluation*, and *result* outlined below.

- *Orientation*: This part of the narrative gives most of the necessary background details and answers the following *wh-* questions: Who? When? What? Where?
- *Complication*: This is the "meat" of the story because it gives most of the details about what happened and usually the problem that occurred, along with any turning point in the story.
- *Evaluation*: This part answers the question: So what? What does the story mean for the participants?
- *Result*: This part outlines and explains the resolution to the problem/crisis.

When you use this adapted framework to situate your story, you can get a clearer hold over what it all means to you, the deeper hidden assumptions you have, as you try to give it some meaning. You can recreate whatever pedagogical actions may have led to the complication you talk about if you give a concise orientation to your story by listing all of the people involved in the story and indicating when and where this story occurred. Only then do you begin to get at the core of the narrative by telling more about what actually happened as you lead into the particular complication. As you begin to evaluate the meaning of the story for your professional lives, you also begin to conceptualize the set of important theoretical issues associated with your story that may have otherwise gone unnoticed. In this way, you can achieve a result that will give you a clearer understanding of your practice, so you can

Reflection Journal 5.5

First, write your own answers to these questions, and then find a partner or a group to discuss your findings and reflections; after these discussions in a pair or group, write a paragraph about your concluding reflections.

- The following teacher narrative was reported by an experienced teacher educator who teaches university-level ESL in Canada, and it reports on her concerns about the negative feedback she received from one of her students after one of her classes. This teacher was part of a group of three ESL university teachers in Canada who collaborated with this author in order to reflect on their practice. The period of reflection was two years and involved weekly group meetings, journal writing, and classroom observations. The information reported in this case study is adapted from a combination of a journal entry she made and what she said about the incident in a group meeting.

  In my class, one of the assessed tasks is called peer teaching. The pre-service teachers present their lesson plan (another assessed task) to the class and teach one or two of the activities or techniques in "teacher-mode" with us role-playing being ESL learners, according to the class profile they have indicated on their lesson plan. Having done this in my TESL classes numerous times, I feel there is a certain value in sharing the lesson plans the pre-service teachers have made while they are trying out their teaching skills. I have an evaluation scheme that assesses the following: use of language, classroom management, knowledge of technique, visual aid, organization and presentation skills. The students know from the second day of classes that this is coming at the end of the term. I model the task for them and I return their lesson plan feedback before they peer teach. I do everything possible to prepare them and make them comfortable, but it still can be slightly stressful for them. This is to be expected I guess.

  Now to the problem, the evaluation and giving feedback: I have, in the past, had to give people feedback about their lessons that they are not happy with – in other words, criticism. Trust me, I do this in the kindest, softest way I can. This week a particular pre-service teacher was not very successful in his peer teaching. This student has been "a question mark" since the beginning of the term. He is intelligent, expresses himself well on paper, and understands the theoretical concepts. His written work has been excellent. He is just not a clear communicator in front of the class. I should also mention that his overall score was not too bad. I felt I was perhaps overly generous in some areas. I had to give him this critical feedback along with some positive feedback. That was fine for me, but he was upset by it. I also had to give him a numerical grade using my scoring key. In the end, I realize that this is his issue and that he needs to behave in a more professional manner. I was not that hard on him.

Actually, as I write this I am already starting to get some ideas. I am also enjoying this and finding it more interesting than my other work that I should be doing right now. One of my TESL students just came in and received her constructive criticism and thanked me for it. It was not a problem! I always start along the lines that I did with him as well, something like, "How do you think it went?" Or "How did you feel?" or something along those lines, something similar to that. It depends on, sometimes I'll say "How did you feel?" or "How do you think it went" depending on the situation. And then he said, he didn't really respond very much to that. I remember that he didn't say anything. And then I kind of probed further and asked him "Were you a bit nervous?" And then he said, "No. Well, maybe a little." He's one of these people, very hard to communicate with.

- Separate this narrative into *Orientation*, *Complication*, and *Evaluation*.
- As part of the result, the teacher in the story above wrote the following:

I now have a number of questions on this issue:

1. Should I give the feedback in a different way? How can I improve in how I do it?
2. Some people accept and enjoy receiving my feedback and see the purpose of why I am doing this while others take it too personally or see it as a personal attack (which it is not).
3. How do I deal with the opposing goals of supportive feedback and evaluation for grades? Should I stop evaluating the peer teaching and just use it as an opportunity for feedback?
4. How can I ensure that all my pre-service teachers see that I am trying to help them, not hinder them?
5. How do I react when I am criticized? Am I so understanding?
6. Why is it when giving ESL students presentation feedback I do not have as much difficulty? How is it different in this case as compared to, for example, after a speaking presentation?
7. When an ESL student takes my feedback overly personally, I do not worry about it too much. I feel that someone who is about to become a teacher needs to know when they are getting constructive criticism and how not to take it too personally. As a teacher myself, I get criticized regularly from a variety of sources, such as ESL course surveys.
8. If a person is not good in front of the class and may not be successful in the ESL teaching classroom because of it, isn't it partially my responsibility to guide them into reflection and improving? Perhaps I just do not like having this responsibility.

- How would you assess each of the eight questions the teacher asked above in relation to her *Result*?
- Are there any other questions this teacher could ask? If so, write them.

achieve fresh perspectives, new insights, and a sense of self-renewal. As mentioned in the chapter on reflective practice, in order to be able to gain this type of insight into the meaning of your professional narratives, you must be able to draw on Dewey's (1933) three attributes of a reflective practitioner, which I think are important to list again here: *open-mindedness*, *responsibility*, and *wholeheartedness*. Open-mindedness means that you should consider different views of what you are reflecting on. Responsibility suggests that you think about the outcomes of your actions before you take them. Wholeheartedness means that you keep trying to make sense of your practice even if you do not get clear answers immediately.

The narrative outlined above demonstrates how real practices can conflict with expectations and outcomes, and, as McCabe (2002: 83) maintains, by analyzing such narratives that conflict with our expectations, "we can come to a greater understanding of the expectations themselves – what our beliefs, philosophies, understandings, conceptions (of the classroom, of the language, of the students, of ourselves) actually are." By reflecting and analyzing the critical incident outlined above, the teacher gained a greater awareness of her practice, which is one of the main goals of reflective practice. Indeed, analyzing critical incidents provides language teachers with further opportunities to consolidate their theoretical understanding of their practices and, as McCabe (2002: 89) has suggested, such analysis can "lead to further exploration of different aspects of teaching through action research."

Writing and Analyzing a Critical Incident

We all have moments in our class that make us stand back for a while because something significant (either positive or negative) has occurred. For example, in a second language class, a student who is normally very shy and hesitant when speaking the second language may one day open up and speak a lot because something has triggered this moment during the lesson. Conversely, a student who is normally active and talkative may one day in class stop talking because of something that occurred during a particular class. Each of these moments or incidents are significant for the teacher because the teacher is taken aback by both of them and forced to reflect while teaching. As Brookfield (1990) has remarked, such critical incidents are vividly remembered events that were never anticipated to happen in the first place. These moments can be very instructive for teachers because if they document and analyze them carefully, they can learn more about themselves as teachers, their assumptions, values, beliefs, and practices. However, just as with the careful documentation of narratives mentioned in the previous section, so must teachers carefully document critical incidents that occur in their classrooms (and indeed outside classrooms) so that they can analyze them carefully as they seek self-renewal. Richards and Farrell (2005) have maintained that by reflecting on these significant events in a formal manner, it may be possible for language teachers to uncover new understandings of the teaching and learning process. This formal approach to reflecting on critical incidents consists of two main phases, namely, a *description/production* phase followed by an *explanation*

Reflection Journal 5.6

First, write your own answers to these questions, and then find a partner or a group to discuss your findings and reflections; after these discussions in a pair or group, write a paragraph about your concluding reflections.

- Read the following critical incidents that were to influence my own approach to language teacher education and classroom observation in particular and my whole approach as a language teacher.

  As a student teacher, I was observed teaching three times by a supervisor from the university where I was a student teacher, and each time I became progressively worse during the class. Having had no pre-observation discussion, the supervisor was already in the classroom each time I got there, seated at the back of the room giving me "The Look" of the expert: "Show me what you can do." I speculated that this might have affected my teaching in a negative way, and having no post-observation conference also may have added to my anxiety. My only feedback from the experience was my final evaluation via the course grade sheet that I received at the end of the year showing that I passed. I now reflect – in part, in reaction to this experience – that in my capacity as a language teacher educator, I always tell my teaching practice students when I am coming to supervise or ask them when they would like me to come visit their class and observe them teach. I also conduct both pre- and post-conference discussions each time I visit. Additionally, I now believe that the learner-teachers have prior experiences that are important, and so they will get no "expert look" from me! I also agree that teacher education programs cannot expect to be effective until they work with the beliefs that guide teachers' actions. I see part of my role as a teacher educator as making these usually tacit prior beliefs explicit to pre-service teachers and then challenging any inconsistencies between previously held beliefs and new knowledge gained from the course. This can be achieved by reflection, and teachers should continually engage in reflective activities so that they can become more aware of who their students are and who they themselves are as teachers.

  - Divide the above critical incident into the *description phase* and the *explanation phase* and then yourself reflect on the explanation.
  - Do you have any series of incidents similar to those of the above writer that you can write about?

phase (Tripp, 1993). It is important not to jump phases and go straight into the explanation phase as many may be tempted to do, without completing the description/production phase. In the description/production phase, some issue has occurred and has been observed by the teacher as being significant; the teacher therefore begins to document the incident in as much detail as possible. The event or incident is thus one in which something the teacher sees as significant has happened. When the incident occurs, it is deemed critical because it interrupts (or highlights) some taken-for-granted ways of thinking about teaching. By analyzing such incidents, teachers can become more aware of the values and beliefs that underpin their teaching practices.

When writing a critical incident, teachers can consider using the following procedures:

1. As a first step, write an account of any "significant incident" from classroom practice (something that happened and that is on your mind), but avoid explanations and interpretations; just include the details of the incident.
2. On a separate page, attempt to explain and interpret the incident. Richards and Farrell (2005) suggest that when reflecting on a critical incident, teachers may want to consider what happened directly before and after each incident as well as their reactions at the time of the incident. Such contextualization may help teachers unpack their underlying assumptions about teaching and learning.
3. Teachers can also adapt McCabe's framework as outlined in this chapter as a means of analyzing their story.
4. Meet with another teacher (a "critical friend" or reflective partner), exchange the first page detailing the incident, and compare your interpretations for the incident with the other person's.
5. These interpretations may provide the basis for further written reflection on the meaning and significance of the original incident, both in the original and other circumstances.

Career Critical Incidents

It is also possible to write and analyze a career critical incident in which something happened while you were teaching or outside the class that caused you to take a course of action later which you may not have in fact planned for had this particular career critical incident not occurred. I remember my friend Harold telling me about a career critical incident that occurred which was the main reason he was sitting beside me a Ph.D. course when I went to the United States to study. Harold was a tenured assistant professor who was teaching in a university setting but who was getting no respect from junior colleagues and could not get any further promotion because he did not have a Ph.D. Harold's critical incident occurred the previous summer when he was walking across his campus one hot summer day while carrying the many papers he had to grade because he was the one person in his department singled out to teach writing to freshmen who had failed their writing course the previous term and had an enormous workload. The critical incident for him was when he tripped and fell, dropping all of the papers and cutting his knee. He decided there and then that he would start another Ph.D. program and finish it this time; earlier in his career he had never finished writing his dissertation in a different Ph.D. program – an all too frequent occurrence. Harold had had enough of the inferior treatment and the subtle insults from his colleagues because he had not acquired a doctoral degree.

Reflection Journal 5.7

First, write your own answers to these questions, and then find a partner or a group to discuss your findings and reflections; after these discussions in a pair or group, write a paragraph about your concluding reflections.

- Reflect on Harold's career-changing critical incident. Why do you think this one event had such an impact on him?
- Do you have any career critical incident that you might want to write up and analyze?
- Do you think this kind of snap decision precipitated by one event is a common thing?

Writing and Analyzing a Case Study

Another means of engaging in narrative inquiry is to reflect on written case studies. Whereas a critical incident is a retrospective analysis of any unexpected incident, a case study starts with the identification of an issue and then the selection of a case-method procedure for reflecting on it (Richards and Farrell, 2005). A case study is like a photograph of an issue that is frozen for reflection later. The issue is identified or relived and then explored for meaning; this reflection can be carried out in writing or as an audio recording. In many instances, a case typifies the sort of dilemma that many teachers may face in their classrooms, and reflecting on such a case can lead to greater self-awareness. When teachers reflect on cases, they can not only learn how to identify important issues in teaching, but also how to frame dilemmas by posing critical questions. Olshtain and Kupferberg (1998: 187) maintain that reflecting on cases allows teachers "to impose order and coherence on the unpredictable classroom reality where there are always alternative solutions to cope with similar problems." In so doing, they can gain more awareness about their underlying assumptions and beliefs about the complex relationship between teaching and learning a second or foreign language.

Reflection Journal 5.8

First, write your own answers to these questions, and then find a partner or a group to discuss your findings and reflections; after these discussions in a pair or group, write a paragraph about your concluding reflections.

Read the following case study (as written by the supervisor based on classroom observation), which features an English language teacher in a Singaporean secondary school teaching a grammar class, and answer the questions that follow. The students in the class were all Chinese and all above average in their English language proficiency. The case study starts with the lesson plan (as presented to the supervisor during a pre-observation conference), then incorporates a report of what the supervisor observed.

CASE STUDY

LESSON PLAN

Topic: Grammar

Duration: 10–10:35 am

Context: Chinese teacher and students in an English lesson in Singapore

Specific Instructional Objectives

At the end of the lesson students will be able to:

- Give proper verb forms for matching subjects (subject–verb agreement, or SVA)

Class Arrangement

Students will be working in pairs

Tuning In (5 mins)

- Students will be shown a few pictures (see Materials) on overhead transparencies (OHTs) or PowerPoint slides (PPs).
- They will be asked to fill in the blanks to complete the sentence which describes the picture, providing each sentence with a subject (*doer*) and a verb (*action word*).
- Mistakes in subject–verb agreement (SVA) will not be corrected at this stage.

LESSON ACTIVITIES (25 mins)

- Students will be shown a few sentences on OHTs/PPs, and they will be asked to identify the doers and actions and to pay attention to SVA.
- In pairs students will be asked to come up with doers and action words. One of the pairs will be asked to give five doers and the other will have to come up with matching actions.
- Examples will be given on OHTs/PPs:

Doers	Actions
John	is eating
The teachers	are walking
Five students	swim
Mr. Lim	laughs

Written Work/Homework (5 mins)

- Each pair will be asked to construct sentences using the doers and action words they came up with during the discussion, paying particular attention to SVA.

Materials

PP presentation/slide show or OHTs with sentences and pictures illustrating these

1. The boy is walking down the slope.
2. John and Sani are singing.
3. One of the teachers eats a lot.
4. The person sitting at the back is sleepy.
5. Mr. and Mrs. James are kind.
6. A bunch of keys was found yesterday.
7. The teacher as well as the students is going home.
8. They visit the retirement home every week.
9. Many students run every morning.
10. The table is expensive.

Classroom Report (written by the supervisor)

The First Five Minutes

The teacher started the class by showing pictures on the OHT. He asked the students to fill in blanks (under the picture on the OHT) for picture # 1. The students shouted out different answers. The teacher said *Ah* as a confirmation response to each answer. Then he wrote in his own answers on the OHT. These answers sometimes agreed with the students' answers. He did not comment on the students' answers directly.

Main Body of Lesson

The teacher continued with the pictures for another five minutes and when he had filled in all the blanks himself, he showed another OHT. Then he wrote the following sentences on the board (he left the OHT on at the same time):

Doers	**Actions**
John	is eating
The teachers	are walking
Five students	swim

Next, the teacher asked his students what part of speech *John* is in the first sentence and what *is eating* is. Some students (in the front of the room) shouted out answers, but most said nothing and were looking at the OHT or out the window. After about ten seconds, the teacher gave a rule for subject–verb agreement. He said, "Subject–verb agreement: A singular subject takes a singular verb." Then he stopped and said, "I now wonder about this rule." He immediately went back to the OHT and asked the students to identify *the doer* and *the action* and the *subject–verb agreement*. He started on the first sentence and asked the students for the answer. One student answered that the *doer* is the boy and the *action* is walking. The teacher did not respond. The teacher then told the students that the subject *boy* agrees with the verb *walking*; however, he did not explain in any way. Then he asked the class to get into pairs and discuss the sentences. This "discussion" lasted about ten minutes. Some of the "pairs" (which really consisted of five or six students, as nobody moved or changed their seats) were talking in Chinese, some sleeping, and only a few were seemingly on task.

The teacher then asked the students to look up at the OHT and to give him some answers. After about ten seconds of silence, the teacher started answering the questions himself, and he underlined the relevant subjects and verbs in each sentence. At the start of each sentence, he asked for answers but never looked up from the OHT or at the pupils. Instead, he continued to write his answers on the OHT, that is, until he got to sentence # 6: *A bunch of keys was found yesterday*. He stopped, looked up and asked for answers. Nobody answered. He did not write anything and began to fumble with his pen. Then he said, "I think that the answer is *A bunch of keys were found*." Then he quickly went to # 7. The teacher said that *the teacher* here is the subject, so *is* is correct. Then the teacher stopped as the buzzer had sounded for the end of the class (meaning five minutes remained until the next class). He then asked the students to make five more examples for the next class for homework.

Post-Class Observation Conference

The observer asked the teacher what he thought about the class – how the teacher thought it went. The teacher responded that he got mixed up with subject–verb agreement concepts in grammar and that he also got mixed up while doing the examples on the OHT. When asked what he thought the students had learned in the lesson, the teacher said he did not know. When asked why he had chosen this particular lesson to teach (subject–verb agreement), the teacher responded that he thought the students needed practice using this structure. However, he did not have any evidence of this from the students' writing or speaking. The observer then asked him what his beliefs were about the place of grammar (including his teaching approach) in English lessons in Singaporean secondary schools. The teacher responded that he really did not know, as this was the first time he had reflected on how to teach grammar in a real class. He said that he had not realized this until the middle of his own class. He said that his main problem during the lesson was: *Should I give the rule or get on with the lesson*? He said he got flustered at the beginning of the class because he realized that he did not know the students' prior experience of subject–verb agreement. He also said that he was not sure of subject–verb agreement as a grammar structure but only realized this when he started to answer the questions he had set for the students. The observer noted that the teacher asked and answered most of his own questions. In response, the teacher said that the students had not answered quickly enough, so he decided to answer for them.

Questions on Case Study

1. Who is involved (in the case)?
2. How is the class organized?
3. What are the objectives of the lesson?
4. What teaching method is tried?
5. How does the teacher view this situation?
6. What actions, if any, are taken to correct this situation?
7. What has the teacher forgotten to take into consideration?
8. What should the teacher do next?

Conclusion

Narrative reflection as discussed in this chapter suggests that language teachers can choose from various means of "imposing order" (Johnson and Golombek, 2002: 4) on their seemingly disparate practices, such by as by writing and analyzing their narratives, writing and analyzing critical incidents, and writing and analyzing case studies describing what occurs in their practice. These forms of reflective writing can cultivate the habit of engaging in reflective practice. In addition, the stories, critical incidents, and case studies outlined in this chapter show how teacher-generated reflective writing can offer a rich source of information about how teachers actually conduct their practices: the thinking and problem-solving they employ, and their underlying assumptions, values, and beliefs.

Chapter 5 Reflections

First, write your own answers to these questions, and then find a partner or a group to discuss your findings and reflections; after these discussions in a pair or group, write a paragraph about your concluding reflections after reading this chapter.

- A study by Golombek and Johnson (2004) involving 3 ESL/EFL teachers focused on teacher-authored narrative inquiry as a tool for professional development. They suggest that such narratives can "help teachers identify contradictions in their teaching" (p. 324).
  - How can narratives help identify contradictions in teaching?
  - How can narratives help teachers better understand themselves as professionals?
  - How can teachers write an action plan based on their understanding of themselves as teachers when reflecting on a case?
  - How can teachers make use of field notes, interviews, journals, letters, autobiographies, and orally told stories to help them construct a case and later reflect on it to gain more self-awareness?

6. Reflecting in the First Year(s) and Beyond

Preamble

So you have secured that first teaching job (you hope!) and you are ready and eager to begin your new role as a language teacher (ESL, EFL, or FL). You are a newly qualified degree holder and teacher, and you are eager to get started. You have lots of ideas that you learned in your teacher education courses and that you are waiting to try out in the classroom, and of course, you are really looking forward to meeting your own students. You enter the school, meet the administrators and other teachers, and you are shown to your classroom after a brief introduction to the school and its policies. You are given a book and course materials and told to "have fun" or "enjoy your classes," or some other positive comments, as you move towards your classroom. You hear the noise from outside as you enter, and suddenly you are in the real world of the second or foreign language classroom.

You soon find out that the real classroom is a bit different from what you were expecting, although you did not really know what to expect. Your teaching practice was in a more protected environment in which a mentor teacher and a supervisor basically told you what to do; and anyway, those were not your students since you were only in the practice classroom for a few weeks. The class starts, and you suddenly realize that this is not as straightforward as you had thought: you find yourself in a fast-paced environment with many things happening at the same time, some of them difficult to control, but you no longer have the back-up you used to have during teaching practice. Now you are on your own; you have to manage the learning environment yourself and make sure you are providing opportunities for your students to learn in a positive classroom context. You begin to feel nervous and isolated, and you wonder if you are alone in your experiences as a novice teacher. You realize that you may not have been adequately prepared for such experiences in your language teacher education courses that gave you a solid background in many theoretical aspects of language teaching and learning. Some of the administrators in your new school/institution may assume that because you have graduated from a certain program and institution with a language teaching or other qualification, you will be able to apply what you have learned during you first year(s) of teaching and beyond. The administrator most likely assumes you are thinking that the educators in these programs and courses would not have educated you in the way they did if what they taught was not going to be of use to you in your future teaching career.

Unfortunately, the reality of a novice teacher's life in the real classroom makes many of the theories and methods they may have learned in their graduate courses unusable. Indeed, more experienced teachers know from their own experiences – and novice teachers may also realize – that the first year and years of teaching can be very difficult and challenging. Thus, novice teachers could do with some help along the way. In fact, the statistics for teachers of whatever subject matter leaving the teaching profession in their first five years is alarming, with some statistics quoting as many as 50% leaving. However, with a certain amount of insight and survival skills, most language teachers can learn how to successfully negotiate their first years and move beyond initial feelings of insecurity to become excellent teachers. This chapter examines some of the challenges that novice language teachers face in their first years in the classroom, and it also examines how teachers can reflect beyond these first years so that they can engage in reflective practice throughout their careers.

Reflection Journal 6.1

First, write your own answers to these questions, and then find a partner or a group to discuss your findings and reflections; after these discussions in a pair or group, write a paragraph about your concluding reflections.

- Most teachers I know remember their first job and their first day in a classroom as a teacher. I do, too. I remember that, after walking into my classroom on the first day in Dublin, Ireland, my major first dilemma was: Do I sit down at the teacher's desk or do I stand up all the time as I teach and if so, where do I stand?
  - Describe your first teaching job after you qualified as a teacher. What made you choose this particular position?
  - Describe your first day in the school/institution. Who met you and who explained what you had to do (if anyone)?
  - What were the biggest differences that you realized on your first day from when you were a graduate student or student teacher?
  - How did you feel after your first day?

Managing in the First Years of Teaching

From Student to Teacher

Many novice teachers enter their first job with considerable idealism about the whole package of teaching that includes learning, students, and instruction in a subject that they are at least interested in and may be passionate about. This idealism was probably formed during their initial graduate program, in which they were exposed to whatever courses a particular group of language educators believed would best prepare them as language experts and teachers. Of course, the operative word here is *believe* because there is not much published research that documents the impact of language teacher education or other graduate programs on the successful socialization of teachers in their first years. In fact, when they enter their new teaching environment as a newly qualified teacher, they more often than not encounter issues and dilemmas that they have not been adequately prepared to meet. Such issues and dilemmas can quickly shatter new teachers' idealism; and if they are not carefully mentored on how to work through these issues, the results can drive them away from a fulfilling life as an educator.

A possible reason for teachers being inadequately prepared for the realities of classroom life that they will face in their first years is that many graduate programs have a strong theoretical focus; and many language teacher education programs focus most of their courses broadly on teaching methods and the institutional context of instruction, rather than on the day to day procedural teaching realities all teachers meet in their work, involving such issues as lesson planning and various aspects of classroom management. It is important for novice teachers to become fully aware of the realities of teaching in a real classroom as early as possible in their career because research has indicated that those who do not receive such help and have an unpleasant experience in

Reflection Journal 6.2

First, write your own answers to these questions, and then find a partner or a group to discuss your findings and reflections; after these discussions in a pair or group, write a paragraph about your concluding reflections.

- Do you think you were adequately prepared as a language teacher for the realities of the classroom you actually encountered?
- Which courses from your graduate program do you think were most helpful, and which were least helpful for you in your first year as a language teacher, and why?
- If you were a director of a language teacher education program, what courses would you make your student-teachers take and why?
- How can we better prepare language teachers for the realities of the classroom they will face?

the first year tend to drop out of the profession. Reflection can go a long way to assisting novice teachers in weathering the first year of teaching.

The Transition: Sink or Swim?

The transition that many novice teachers make from the teacher education program to the real life of the classroom has been called "reality shock" (Veenman, 1984) because the idealism mentioned above can be shattered by many competing issues and dilemmas that the novice has to deal with all at the same time. Many of these challenges happen within the classroom during the course of a teaching day and require immediate attention and many kinds of classroom management. Other challenges wait outside the classroom, such as having to fit into a new subculture of teaching with established colleagues. The latter challenge is often overlooked in teacher education programs, although it is an important issue in first-year teacher development. Fitting in with new colleagues is not always easy, and several different "teacher cultures" or groups may exist in one school, so that novice teachers are faced with a dilemma of which one, if any one, to join (Carew and Lightfoot, 1979). The culture of any school in which a beginning teacher works usually exists on a continuum from a highly individualistic school culture, in which teachers "do their own thing," to a collaborative culture in which the teachers are willing to help one another. Indeed, Lortie (1975: 195) has provided evidence that in some schools, so-called collegial relationships can best be characterized as "live and let live, and help when asked." This kind of "live and let live" collegial culture can be a problem when a novice teacher goes to the staff room or teachers' lounge to get some guidance from other teachers or the administration. The novice soon realizes that such guidance is not readily available and that the new teacher is pretty much on his or her own, operating in a type of "sink-or-swim" experience (Varah, Theune, and Parker, 1986). So what is a new teacher to do?

Each school should have an induction or orientation program for all teachers new to that school (either novice or experienced) so that they can be socialized properly into school culture. Bliss and Reck (1991: 6) define *teacher socialization* as "the process by which an individual becomes a participating member of the society of teachers." The operative word in this definition is *participating*, but many schools think this means also fully functional, regardless of one's experience or lack thereof. After all, the logic goes, we pay the teachers, they are supposed to be qualified, and we have explained everything to them in our induction/orientation program that we gave them on the first day; so they should be able to teach a full load. Although there seems to be a growing awareness among educators in some countries (e.g. the United Kingdom and the United States) that teachers in their first years benefit from support in the form of reduced teaching loads and the appointment of mentors to help the teacher, this may not be the case in other countries and educational settings (especially in economically difficult times). The usual induction/orientation program includes pamphlets that outline the school rules and regulations, along with other school documents that explain aspects of the school system to the new teacher. At best, these are reviewed with the teacher in a session introducing the overall school culture; but all too often they are simply handed to the new teacher to read in his or her "free time." Indeed, some have pointed out that in the private sector workplace (usually in private language schools), qualified teachers in their first years may not be offered any type of orientation or a period of induction, and as a result, after one or two years of teaching, these novice teachers may experience severe feelings of inadequacy because of their unfulfilled expectations, especially if they are properly qualified. (I realize some of these unfulfilled expectations may be the result of other issues individual and personal to each teacher and thus not related to any induction program.) Eventually, many of these teachers become cynical about the whole experience and because they have not been mentored in any way, they tend to burn out quickly and eventually leave teaching. Administrators in some (not all) private language schools take the view that novice teachers

Reflection Journal 6.3

First, write your own answers to these questions, and then find a partner or a group to discuss your findings and reflections; after these discussions in a pair or group, write a paragraph about your concluding reflections.

- Describe your induction or orientation into your first or most recent school or department. Was it an official or an unofficial program?
- What literature did you get about the school/department and your particular duties (if any)?
- Who explained to you details about the students you would be teaching and the material you would be using (if anyone)?
- Were you assigned anyone to help guide you through your first week, month, or year?
- Did you have an official mentor or an informal buddy, both, or none?
- What would be the role of a mentor or buddy for a novice teacher in his or her first year?
- Why would the first year(s) of teaching be a sink-or-swim type of experience for novice teachers?
- Which type of school (including colleges and universities) would it be easier for a novice teacher to "sink" in, and which type of school would it be easier for a novice teacher to "swim" in, a private or a state-run school, and why?
- What type of "teacher cultures" may exist in different schools?
- Describe the "teacher culture" in your present school.
- Why would some schools have a culture of "live and let live, and help when asked"?

are especially glad to have a job, and they will pay them at the lowest salary possible but give them a full teaching load so that they can get the most out of them as soon as possible (or, as one administrator admitted to me, "before they become too cynical about the whole thing!").

In sum, many novice teachers maybe be swimming in their first days, but they are surely headed for choppy waters that will eventually lead them to sink unless they receive some guidance in the early part of their careers. Whose responsibility should this be? Who should lead the guidance? I will address this question in the section on mentors that follows.

The Mentor

Of the schools that do take an interest in helping novice teachers, some appoint an official mentor for novice teachers while others ask a senior teacher to "look after" a novice teacher when the teacher arrives; unfortunately, there are other schools which just leave the novice teacher to his or her own devices from the first day. Even if a mentor is appointed, it may be more or less effective. This appointment can be made from the ranks of senior teachers or whomever is available at the time the novice walks in the door. I have seen a case in one school where the teacher who was asked to act as mentor was a novice herself the previous year and had in fact graduated only the year prior to that. I have also seen experienced mentors who did not work out well, for various reasons. Thus, the appointment of a mentor teacher to a novice in his or her first year is no guarantee that the mentoring arrangement will work.

That said, most researchers on first year language teacher development agree on one issue: that novice teachers need assistance and lots of support in the first year (Farrell, 2008a, 2009). This support, especially in the skills of teaching and especially of the emotional kind, can come from colleagues within the school and from the school administration. Colleagues' support and assistance is very important for the successful development of novice teachers in their first years. As Williams, Prestage, and Bedward (2001: 256–257) caution, if a novice teacher's colleagues pursue a culture of individualism (as opposed to collaboration), this will be " at worst, potentially damaging to the NQT's [newly qualified teacher's] development and at best, damaging to the longer term interests of the school." The school administration can help with this development of collegiality by encouraging mentoring of novice teachers and by officially appointing a mentor teacher for the novice teacher. A mentor teacher in this case is "a knowledgeable person [who] aids a less knowledgeable person" (Eisenman and Thornton, 1999: 81). This type of mentoring is well-established as a support system for novice teachers in many Western educational settings. Since the mid-1980s, induction programs in the United States, for example, have increasingly provided assistance to new teachers by assigning them to mentors. These mentor teachers have usually been drawn from veteran teachers within a school who help beginners learn the philosophy, cultural values, and established sets of behaviors expected by the schools employing them. Concerned about the rate of attrition during the first three years of teaching and aware of the problems faced by beginning teachers, educators saw the logic of providing onsite support and assistance to novices during their first year of teaching. Research indicated that beginning teachers who are mentored are more effective teachers in their early years, since they learn from guided practice rather than depending too much upon trial-and-error efforts. It was found that mentored novice teachers tend to leave the teaching profession at a lower rate than non-mentored novices.

Reflection Journal 6.4

First, write your own answers to these questions, and then find a partner or a group to discuss your findings and reflections; after these discussions in a pair or group, write a paragraph about your concluding reflections.

- Why would mentored teachers tend to leave the teaching profession at a lower rate than non-mentored teachers?
- Describe the mentoring you received when you were a novice teacher.
- Who appointed your mentor (assuming a mentor was appointed), and what was the process?
- Within language teaching, Malderez and Bodoczky (1999: 4) have described five different roles that mentors can play:
  1. A *model* who inspires and demonstrates;
  2. An *acculturator* who provides a clear understanding of the educational system;
  3. A *sponsor* who introduces the student teacher to the appropriate people;
  4. A *supporter* who acts as sounding board and provides safe opportunities for the student teacher to discuss teaching practices;
  5. An *educator* who facilitates pedagogical ideas to help the student teacher achieve professional learning objectives.
- Which, if any, of these roles did your mentor play during your first year?
- Was your mentor clear or unclear about the role he or she was asked to play?
- Was your mentor able to explain clearly how you could be successful in that school?
- What training or experience would a mentor need to have before he or she could successfully help a novice teacher adjust to school life?

Novice Teacher Development

Imagine that you have survived the first days and even your first month as a novice teacher and now you are becoming a bit more settled in your new role. You are beginning to notice some patterns, many of which still remain unclear. You are beginning to come out of your survival mode during that first month and you are beginning to come to terms with the reality of teaching: it is much different than what you expected and what you trained for. You are finally beginning to make that transition from the ideals you built up during your teacher education program to the reality of school and classroom life, that is, your real world of teaching.

Some educational researchers suggest that teachers go through particular stages during their first year as a teacher, moving in the beginning from a focus on the self and survival to more of a focus on their students as they become more confident about their teaching. It has also been noted that the process of moving through these stages is idiosyncratic because no two teachers develop at the same pace. Their early idealism has the beginning teacher strongly identifying with the students while rejecting the image of the older cynical teacher. In the survival stage, the beginning teacher reacting to the reality shock of the classroom and feels overwhelmed by the complexity of the teaching. The beginning teacher wants to survive with quick-fix methods. The next stage of development, according to Maynard and Furlong (1995), is when the beginning teacher gains an awareness of the difficulties of teaching and begins to recognize that teachers are limited in terms of what they can achieve. At that point, the teacher enters a self-doubt stage and wonders if he or she can make it as a teacher. Beginning teachers then enter a stage known as "reaching a plateau" (Maynard and Furlong, 1995: 13), when they start coping successfully with the routines of teaching; as Maynard and Furlong (1995: 13) observed: "at last they have found a way of teaching that seems to work and they are going to stick to it." However, at this stage, they also develop a resistance to trying new approaches and methods so as not to upset the newly developed routines. At this plateau stage, they are focused on successful classroom management and not so much on student learning. This later changes, however, to more of a focus on the quality of student learning as the beginning teacher moves into a "moving on" stage of development. Maynard and Furlong (1995) suggest that the beginning teacher needs a lot of support at this stage or s/he will not be able to develop further as a result of possible burnout.

Not all researchers agree that beginning teachers move cleanly through phases or stages as they learn how to teach. Bullough and Baughman (1993), for example, have cautioned against the idea that teachers move through stages as they develop. They suggest that when "learning to teach, one encounters problems in clusters not rows.... [S]tages inevitably introduce distortion, an

Reflection Journal 6.5

First, write your own answers to these questions, and then find a partner or a group to discuss your findings and reflections; after these discussions in a pair or group, write a paragraph about your concluding reflections.

- What impact (if any) did your graduate language or teacher education program and each specific course) have on you in your first year(s)?
- What courses from this program do you remember now because of their relevance?
- What stages of development do you think novice teachers go through during their first year(s) language teachers?
- Maynard and Furlong (1995: 12–13) have suggested that novice teachers go through five stages of development: (1) early idealism, (2) survival, (3) recognizing difficulties, (4) reaching a plateau, and (5) moving on.
  - Outline what you think happens or should happen at each stage.
  - Describe how you did or did not proceed in relation to these stages during your first year.
- The following comments (adapted from Richards and Farrell, 2011) reflect some of the problems experienced by teachers in their first year of teaching. Comment on each of these and say if you have had similar issues to deal with in your first years.
  - *I discovered during my first year of teaching that part of the challenge was all about keeping some sense of balance, or indeed, finding my own balance because there are so many issues thrown at you and you do not have the support or protection you had while doing teaching practice.*
  - *During my first year, I had lots of problems related to my new colleagues in the school because they thought I was a bit too eager with everything and that I was showing them up (or trying to).*
  - *When I entered my new institution for my full-time job, I was just thrown into the class without any formal process of induction beyond an initial meeting with the institution head. In fact, we did not have any staff meeting for the first 7 weeks of school.*
  - *Because I am a non-native English speaking ESL teacher, my first year was full of self-doubt and I lacked self-confidence because of my perceived limited professional competence. My experiences concerning discrimination in hiring practices that relate directly to language proficiency in that school did not help me settle at all.*
  - *During my first year of teaching, I had to completely forget what I learned in teaching practice and the teacher education program because of the complete domination of the culture of examinations that overly influenced teaching approaches in that school.*
- Now write your own short teaching story about your first-year or other new-school experience.

old criticism of stage theories that ought to be kept in mind" (Bullough and Baughman, 1993: 94). The jury is still out as to whether "stages" or "clusters" best describe the problems newly qualified teachers encounter in their first year(s); but one thing is for sure: these novice teachers will encounter some problems that will need to be solved while they are teaching rather than afterwards with a supervisor, as they experienced during their practicum. And because they are in a real classroom teaching real students, these novice teachers will have to solve these problems in real time. Given these realities of teaching, graduate language and teacher education programs, with cooperation and collaboration from the schools themselves, will have to work harder at preparing language teachers with the necessary tools to succeed in their first years.

New teachers will probably experience all kinds of different emotions, including frustration, enjoyment, excitement, anxiety, and many other emotions, as they go through these early years in the classroom. To make sure they reach at least stage four (plateauing), and preferably to the "moving on" stage as well, in Maynard and Furlong's (1995) development stage theory, teacher educators must have some sort of back-up built into the system to help new teachers better achieve a level where they are comfortable that they are doing their best for their students in each class they prepare for and will eventually have to deliver instruction in the most professional manner possible. This cannot all be left to chance under the assumption that because the novice teacher has finished their graduate course, s/he can implement some ideas from these courses without any kind of follow-up. Indeed, some teachers (and teachers who are in their first years seem to be the most vocal in this) question the validity of the impact of teacher education courses on the real world of teaching. I will address this point in the section that follows.

The Impact of the Teacher Education Program

Imagine that you are developing well now and have become a bit more settled in your new role as a full-time teacher. You are beginning to notice patterns about your role both inside and outside the classroom, and you are even beginning to notice the impact of your teacher education courses, in that you can implement some theories or methods and techniques while others you cannot. Now you are beginning to question what you learned in your graduate program, and you are beginning to wonder what ideals, theories, and techniques you can hold onto; which ones you must modify; and which ones you cannot use at all.

Language teaching research has indicated there are conflicting results on what first-year teachers actually implement from their teacher preparation courses when they teach in a real context for the first time. For example,

Richards and Pennington's (1998) study of first-year English language teachers in Hong Kong revealed that most seemed to completely abandon or ignore many of the principles from their teacher education program. Indeed, Tarone and Allwright (2005: 12) have maintained that the differences between the academic course content in language teacher preparation programs and the real conditions that novice teachers are faced with in the language classroom in their first year appears to "set up a gap that cannot be bridged by beginning teacher learners." So there are some issues still to be resolved between what language teacher educators provide in teacher preparation courses and what actually occurs in real classrooms. Some of these issues could probably be better addressed with more anticipatory reflective practice courses (such as reflecting on future practice) that prepare teachers for what they may encounter rather than not addressing this at all. In addition, language teacher educators could remain in contact with their newly qualified teachers and continue to act as a mentor by having the NQT document his/her experiences during the first year(s) of teaching. In this way, both the NQT and the teacher educator can benefit: the NQT can continue to receive feedback even though the practicum has ended, and the teacher educator can use the information from the NQT's experiences as a case study for teachers who have not yet qualified. In addition, language teacher educators should make greater efforts to develop their courses in relation to the real contexts of teaching rather than the influence of some senior colleagues who may emphasize theory over practice or want to teach subjects or topics that they are interested in rather than what will be useful for their graduates.

Unfortunately, it seems that the formulation of graduate language teacher preparation courses are, to a greater or lesser degree, devised according to the self-interest of faculty members rather than what would be in the best interests of their students. Things are not helped when language teacher education programs are housed in different colleges, departments, or faculties worldwide, as this discourages uniform standards. In addition, because many who teach in graduate language teacher certification or Masters programs have never themselves experienced life as a classroom language teacher, they have no clear understanding of what will be needed by these graduates once they face the reality of their language teaching classrooms. It would therefore be a good idea for people who teach these courses to experience such classrooms and to make real efforts to derive practical instruction from that experience. One way of accomplishing this is to have the professors observe or co-teach courses in language schools or departments that are attached to the university or that exist in the wider community.

Reflection Journal 6.6

First, write your own answers to these questions, and then find a partner or a group to discuss your findings and reflections; after these discussions in a pair or group, write a paragraph about your concluding reflections.

- Why do you think there is a "gap" between teacher education programs and the reality of a school classroom?
- Can you describe or graph this gap?
- How do you think we can fill in this gap?
- Why would a teacher hold onto his/her long-standing (from student days) methodological values while teaching in the first year even though s/he has taken courses to prepare as a teacher that may offer different values? In other words, why would the teacher not change as a result of the courses?
- What situations would make a teacher completely abandon or ignore many of the principles from their graduate program when they enter a classroom for the first time?
- What values did you change as a result of taking a teacher education or other graduate program?
- What values did you keep, and why?
- Do you think language teacher educators should have experience as teachers in real language teaching classrooms before they are allowed to teach in a teacher preparation program?
- Below, I briefly outline a case study of a beginning English language teacher's efforts to hold onto methodological values that he acquired in his teacher education methods courses, in spite of the realities of his context that emphasized more traditional approaches and methods to teaching English language. Read the discussion and then answer the questions that follow.

Jeremy had qualified as an English language teacher after a ten-month course and then went to a school to teach English language after successfully completing his teaching practice. This reflection activity focuses on his approach to teaching reading. In one English language reading class during his first year, Jeremy was trying to include his students' perceptions of the effectiveness of particular reading strategies during the lesson. Jeremy started the class by recapping what they had done the day before, as outlined in Episode 1 below.

Episode 1

Jeremy: What we have done is started from the first paragraph. How many times have you read this? Twice. The first time is skimming for a chain of events. Now look at the questions [in the text].

The teacher then asked the questions, which recapped the events of the reading in chronological order, and all the students answered the questions with little difficulty. This was after only one time reading [compared to the suggested two times which he had outlined as a preferred strategy in the previous lesson]. One student then said he knew why they were able to understand and answer the questions:

Student (male): I know why we know the answers. You [teacher] went through the chain of events with us, so it was easy.

The student was implying that he would not have been able to answer the questions without the previous lesson when the teacher highlighted certain strategies, such as noting the chain of events.

Jeremy: Yes (emphatically), that is what I am doing with you (smiling).

Jeremy then showed the chain of events, listing them one by one as 13 points, on the OHT. Next, he asked the students their opinion of this method:

Jeremy: How many think this is a better way than the others I have shown you?
Ss: (All students put hands up.)
Jeremy: How many think this takes more effort?
Ss: (Half the students' hands up.)
Jeremy: You have a test in two weeks; please try this – better than reading over and over. Let's try difficult questions.

By trying out different methods, the teacher had found his own way, his teaching self, and a self that suited his context, his students, and his developing teaching style. He was trying to match theory and practice even though he may have felt constrained by institutional directives and rules. The school principal, who had observed Jeremy teaching on two occasions during his first year, also endorsed this opinion. He noted that the teacher was trying to be more interactive as the year progressed and said that towards the end of the semester, "he was most impressed with the way the teacher was so pupil-centered."

- Do you think Jeremy was successful or not in maintaining his methodological values? Why or why not?
- What would you have done?

Reflecting Beyond First Year(s)

Why do those of us who have been teaching for years need to reflect after years of teaching? Surely we know it all by now. After all, we have been doing the same thing for years now: the same techniques, the same jokes, the same homework, and we know it inside and out. And therein lies the problem: we have been doing the same thing so long that we do not even know what it is we do anymore. We may think we know what we do, but we may in fact be doing something completely different. In other words, our beliefs and practices may not match anymore.

In fact, it is all too true that some teachers tend to apply some of the techniques they learned in some of their initial teacher education courses during their first years and then continue with those techniques for the remainder of their teaching careers without much reflection. This application of "tried and trusted" methods occurs throughout these teachers' careers, regardless of advances in our profession. They think that once they have studied and graduated, they do not have to study anymore. However, the knowledge base of language teaching has expanded to include much more now than say ten years ago, and these advances should be taken on board by reflective teachers. Let us take as an example a graduate degree in Applied Linguistics now and ten years ago. Nowadays such a degree might include courses in sociolinguistics, psycholinguistics, and second language acquisition; and the unitary teaching methods course of ten years ago has often been divided into separate courses in grammar, writing, listening, speaking, reading, and possibly phonology, too, as the knowledge base within these subskills of language teaching has exploded. Although such courses are typical in Applied Linguistics graduate programs, it is in fact difficult to find two graduate programs that offer the same courses.

Reflection Journal 6.7

First, write your own answers to these questions, and then find a partner or a group to discuss your findings and reflections; after these discussions in a pair or group, write a paragraph about your concluding reflections.

- What are the main developments within your field that you have noticed in the last ten or twenty years?
- How do you keep up with new developments in your field?
- How do you think language teachers should keep up with the changes in their profession?

Reflecting Beyond First Year(s): An Example

The following is a brief report on of a case study of a group of six mid-career English language teachers in Singapore as they reflected on their teaching of English reading and especially about how they teach reading to elementary school students (Devi, 2002). This report focuses on the differences between their stated beliefs during various group meetings and face-to-face interviews and their observed actual classroom practices: the teachers were observed over six classroom lessons each. The group of six teachers were very eager to reflect on their practices concerning teaching reading to their students as they had been doing this for some time now, and when they were asked if they wanted to all join together to form a teacher reflection group in the same school, they jumped at the opportunity not only to talk about their own classes but also to listen to other teachers' ideas. The group had a facilitator who organized the logistics of the meetings and facilitated the discussions, interviews, and classroom observations. All of these were recorded and later transcribed so that the findings could be triangulated. Later, these transcriptions were coded and the findings were then run by the teachers for their comments. A summary of the findings is shown below in Table 6.1, as the teachers' stated beliefs about their teaching of reading.

Table 6.1 Summary of teachers' beliefs (adapted from Devi, 2002: 80).

		Teacher					
	Beliefs	A	B	C	D	E	F
1	The provision of interesting materials helps motivate the students.	✓	✓	✓	✓	✓	✓
2	Stories introduced should be short and predictable.	✓	✓	✓	✓	✓	✓
3	The vocabulary used in the stories should be controlled in terms of the frequency and difficulty level.	✓	✓	✓	✓	✓	✓
4	The book must be attractive and well-illustrated.	✓	✓	✓	✓	✓	✓
5	Instruction on vocabulary is essential to help students to read.	✓	×	✓	✓	×	×
6	Students need to be taught phonemic awareness strategies.	✓	×	×	×	×	×
7	Peer coaching helps students to read.	×	×	×	×	×	✓
8	Collaborative learning strategies help create a safe climate for learning to read.	×	×	✓	×	×	×

KEY: ✓ stated; ×: not stated

As can been seen in Table 6.1 above, eight stated beliefs emerged from the group discussions, and these covered part of each of the six teachers' stated belief systems. These eight beliefs concerning the teaching of reading were as follows:

1. The provision of interesting materials helps motivate the students.
2. Stories introduced should be short and predictable.
3. The vocabulary used in the stories should be controlled in terms of the frequency and difficulty level.
4. The book must be attractive and well-illustrated.

5. Instruction on vocabulary is essential to help students to read.
6. Students need to be taught phonemic awareness strategies.
7. Peer coaching helps students to read.
8. Collaborative learning strategies help create a safe climate for learning to read.

As can be seen in Table 6.1, no teacher explicitly held all of these beliefs, but all of the teachers explicitly held the first four beliefs and half held the fifth one, while each of the last three of the listed beliefs was held by only one teacher. The facilitator then observed each of the six teachers while they were teaching reading classes. Table 6.2 below gives a summary of the teachers` observed classroom practices.

Table 6.2 Summary of teachers' actual classroom practices (adapted from Devi, 2002: 81).

		Teacher					
S/N	Actual classroom practices	A	B	C	D	E	F
1	Interesting materials are used.	✓	✓	✓	✓	✓	✓
2	Stories introduced are short and predictable.	✓	✓	✓	✓	✓	✓
3	The vocabulary used in the stories are controlled in terms of the frequency and difficulty level.	✓	✓	✓	✓	✓	✓
4	The books used are attractive and well-illustrated.	✓	✓	✓	✓	✓	✓
5	Instruction on vocabulary is made explicit.	✓	✓	✓	✓	×	×
6	Students are taught phonemic awareness strategies.	×	×	×	×	×	×
7	Peer coaching is introduced to help weak readers.	×	×	×	×	×	✓
8	Collaborative learning strategies are used to help create a safe climate for learning to read.	×	×	✓	×	×	×
9	Meaning-based strategies are used to help students construct meaning.	✓	✓	✓	✓	✓	✓

KEY: ✓ Observed; × not observed

If you compare the two tables above, or if you compare the teachers' stated beliefs and their actual classroom practices, the results indicate a pretty close match but also some differences between what the teachers say they do when teaching reading and what they actually do in the classroom. For example, it seems that all of the teachers used interesting materials, short and predictable stories, controlled vocabulary, and attractive and well-illustrated books, thus matching the groups' stated beliefs. However, they all also used meaning-based strategies for teaching reading lessons when they were in class, but these had not come out as part of their stated belief systems during group discussions or individual interviews. Looking for example at Teacher B, she used two additional approaches when teaching reading, namely, vocabulary instruction and the use of meaning-based strategies, that she had not mentioned within her stated belief system for teaching reading, even though she was asked to outline what methods she made use of in her classes when teaching reading both in the group discussions and in her individual interviews. Teacher C also used two techniques, collaborative strategies and meaning-based strategies, not mentioned in her beliefs interview, while teachers A, D, and E used one technique, that of meaning-based strategies, not mentioned in their beliefs discussion or interview. The trend that is most noticeable from the comparison across the six teachers is that there is a discrepancy between the teachers' stated beliefs and their actual practices with regard to learning to read through the use of meaning-based strategies. None of the six teachers had mentioned the use of this approach as a belief they advocated. However, all of them used this approach in all six of their observed lessons.

It is interesting to note that the six teachers in this study said that they seldom, if ever, had the opportunity to talk to other teachers and to interact professionally on issues like the teaching of reading. They noticed that the group discussions and the varied perspectives they got from each member of the group enabled them to reflect on the differences between their espoused teaching theories (their stated beliefs) and their teaching theories in action (their classroom practices). When the results of the study were shared with these teachers, they realized that what they thought they were doing in class and what they were actually doing was somewhat different. These interactions with their peers led them on the path to further reflections on their actions. Moreover, it seems that the increased professional interactions that took place led to enhanced professional interactions between these teachers and other colleagues in the school. All six teachers noted that they were able to talk about similarities and differences regarding their approaches to teaching reading and that this opportunity enabled them to obtain a deeper understanding of themselves, their own professional development needs, and the professional needs of their colleagues.

I have found similar results when I have been asked by various teachers to observe them as they teach. For example, some teachers tell me they are learner-centered in their approach to their classes, but when I observe them teach, I see them standing up front and center in the classroom, usually speaking 90% of the total talking time in class. Learner-centered approaches in language classrooms try to have students talk at least the same amount of time that the teacher is talking, that is, more a 50–50 split of total talking time.

Reflection Journal 6.8

First, write your own answers to these questions, and then find a partner or a group to discuss your findings and reflections; after these discussions in a pair or group, write a paragraph about your concluding reflections.

- Look at the six teachers' stated beliefs and comment on each one as it relates to the teaching of reading. What are your beliefs about teaching reading in a second language? How similar are they to those outlined above?
- Look at the teachers' actual classroom practices and comment on each one as it relates to the teaching of reading. What are your classroom practices regarding the teaching of reading? How similar are they to those outlined above?
- Have you ever participated in a teacher group in order to reflect on your work?
- If not, how would you go about setting up such a group?

Moving On

If we consider teaching a profession, then we can say that all teachers have careers that span many years and that during their careers, they go through different stages of development, which sometimes (but not always) result in observable and overt changes in their classrooms. This is sometimes called a teacher's *career life cycle*. According to Huberman's (1993) model, which is based on the study of 160 Swiss high school teachers, teachers go through a range of different stages, starting with a *career entry* stage when teachers begin to teach and experience some discomfort as they attempt to survive the initial joys and pains of learning to teach. They then move on to a *stabilization* stage, in that they decide to stick with teaching and become committed to this as a career, mainly because they are now comfortable as a teacher both inside and outside the classroom. With this increased level of comfort, they now also enter an *experimentation* stage when they try different approaches and methods together with different instructional materials. This experimentation stage can coincide with a *diversification* stage when teachers sometimes look for more responsibility within the context they are teaching in the form of a leadership position – but not all teachers look for this. Sometimes, too, at this stage teachers can become disillusioned with teaching as they allow self-doubt to enter their teaching thoughts, if they perceive that their teaching and daily life in the classroom has become monotonous for them. This may lead to a *reassessment* stage because they begin to look at everything associated with their professional lives. If teachers come out of this intact, then they enter a *serene, affective* stage in which they become more self-sufficient because they have become more confident in what they want to achieve during their career.

Huberman (1993) suggests, though, that this stage can also be accompanied with a declining sense of personal ambition and may lead to a further stage, *conservatism*, that breeds resistance, increased complaints, an overall sense of rigidity, and even some bitterness because of a perceived sense of loss on the part of the teacher. Thankfully, not many teachers end up in this stage; but if they do, they can enter into a more dangerous final stage of *disengagement*, in which they retire on the job because they have withdrawn from most of their professional commitments. Such disengagement may result in a teacher who is completely happy and serene or one who is totally bitter and angry at the end of his/her career.

Reflection Journal 6.9

First, write your own answers to these questions, and then find a partner or a group to discuss your findings and reflections; after these discussions in a pair or group, write a paragraph about your concluding reflections.

- Look at Huberman's stage model above and comment on each stage.
- Do you agree with this model?
- Do you know anyone who is at the *conservatism* stage "that breeds resistance, increased complaints, an overall sense of rigidity, and even some bitterness"?
- Do you see yourself at any of these stages (more than one can be possible)?
- Would you add any more stages that could be specific to language teachers?
- Do you think language teachers move through these stages in linear fashion (from one to the next), or do you think teachers can experience more than one stage at the same time and even return to a previous stage?
- Do you think that language teaching is a vocation (i.e. a deliberate career choice for you) or something else?
- Do you think that language teachers have the same career advancement (progression through the ranks) as other teachers?
- Do you think that the model presented above covers such issues as a teacher's demotivation because of excessive workloads and poor administration that are prevalent in language teaching contexts (see Skinner, 2002)?
- Would you leave the language teaching profession if you got a "better" offer and if so, what would that "better" offer be? Why or why not would you leave?
- Do you think that language teachers who teach in their own country (e.g. ESL) are different from language teachers who teach in a different country (e.g. EFL) in terms of their commitment, career paths, and overall lifestyle as a teacher?

Conclusion

Reflective practice can be difficult for teachers in their first years because they are bombarded with many different issues all at one time as they make the transition from their teacher education programs to the reality of a classroom and full-time job. This means that novice teachers may find it difficult to reflect as they teach (reflection-in-action) because they may just be trying to survive. Novice teachers can however reflect on their actions after the teaching event by any of the modes of reflection already discussed in previous chapters. As they gain more experience and begin to move on with their teaching career, they begin to gain more confidence in their abilities and those of their students. Moving on for most teachers means that they need to continuously reflect on their practice while they are developing and throughout their careers,

Chapter 6 Reflections

First, write your own answers to these questions, and then find a partner or a group to discuss your findings and reflections; after these discussions in a pair or group, write a paragraph about your concluding reflections after reading this chapter

- If you were starting off in a school for the first time, what is the most important information you would need to know, and why?
- Who would you ask to get this information?
- Richards and Farrell (2011) say that teaching involves understanding the dynamics and relationships within the classroom and the rules and behaviors specific to a particular setting. For this reason, teaching is sometimes described as a "situated" activity. Schools have their own ways of doing things. In some schools, textbooks are the core of the curriculum, and teachers follow a prescribed curriculum. In others, teachers work from course guidelines and implement them as they see fit. How would you go about getting more information about your context as a novice teacher?
- What advice would you give a novice teacher starting in your school?
- How would you explain the "culture(s) of teachers" existing in your school?
- Vidya, an ESL teacher in Canada said the following: *I have worked in two different institutions in the past. The work cultures in the two places were almost opposite to one another. The personality of the head of the institutions had a lot to do in shaping the working environment in both. In the first place, there was hardly any discipline in the campus and most of the senior members of the staff dominated the juniors. The next institution was headed by a strict principal, who nevertheless was a great teacher. So the whole working atmosphere was student-centered.*
  - How can a new teacher adjust to different school cultures or indeed, should a new teacher adjust to different school culture?

or risk falling into teaching routines that have unknown consequences for their students' learning. The next chapter (Chapter 7) outlines and discusses how and what language teachers have been reflecting on at different times in their careers.

7. Reflecting For Action

Preamble

I remember when I was teaching in Korea, one teacher there who was helping with an ESL teaching journal asked me one day to consider writing something for the journal. I was astonished that he would ask me to write as I was a "nobody" and never once considered this idea before then. I remember at the time thinking that the only people I thought should write were the ones writing the textbooks. What did I know, as I was only a classroom teacher. He kept after me, however, and eventually I did write for the journal; I think my first piece was about how to teach listening using "soap operas" on television. I worked very hard on that piece, and I remember that I was very anxious when I gave it to him. He thanked me and said I would be notified when it was to be published. I wondered if he was mistaken and should have said *if* rather than *when* it was to be published. A few weeks later, I saw my first ever paper in print, and with very few changes. I was amazed and of course delighted because (a) someone would ask me to write, (b) someone would publish what I wrote, and (c) another someone would read it. Why my reluctance and why the reluctance of many practicing language teachers to write about their practice?

Often language teachers think either that they have nothing to say about their teaching or that what they have to say is of little significance to other teachers or language educators. Indeed, one main issue over the years with language educators has been how to encourage language teachers to articulate their "inner world of choices made in response to the outer world of the teaching context" (Mann, 2005: 105) in order to fully account for a knowledge base of language teaching. This is important because regardless of what language educators say language teachers should be doing in their classrooms, it is you, the practicing teacher, who has the final say about what you do in the classroom each day and how you do it. Therefore, it would be best for all concerned – language educators, administrators, and teachers – to know and understand what is actually happening in everyday language classrooms.

Reflection Journal 7.1

First, write your own answers to these questions, and then find a partner or a group to discuss your findings and reflections; after these discussions in a pair or group, write a paragraph about your concluding reflections.

- Do you think you have anything to share with other teachers about your practice?
- What would you look at in your teaching if you were given time, and why?
- How would you go about looking at this?

One way of gathering detailed accounts about the choices, decisions, beliefs, and classroom practices that language teachers make each day is to encourage teachers to engage in some form of systematic reflective practice throughout their careers and to turn this reflection into teacher research. Some scholars have noted that when teachers engage in research, they are becoming more aware of what they do and the ways this impacts how their students learn. Achieving this level of awareness is one of the main purposes of engaging in reflective practice (Farrell, 2007). I was fortunate to have been chosen as the series editor for the Language Teacher Research Series by the TESOL organization, and this series provides the majority of the examples of language teachers' writing and reflecting on their practice in this chapter. The TESOL series was developed so that language teachers could have a forum to share research on their practice in their own contexts. The idea was that contributors would not only deepen their individual understanding of what they do but, more importantly, they would have a way to share their findings with many other language teachers. The series attempted to cover as many geographic regions as possible, representing the Americas, Asia, Europe, the Middle East, Australia/New Zealand, and Africa. What is distinctive about this series is that these studies document how individual language teachers at all levels of practice systematically reflect on their own practice. This is very different from what has been the standard in language research conducted by outside academics who attempt to interpret other teachers' practices even

Reflection Journal 7.2

First, write your own answers to these questions, and then find a partner or a group to discuss your findings and reflections; after these discussions in a pair or group, write a paragraph about your concluding reflections.

- What does the concept of language teacher research mean to you?
- Do you think teachers should be consumers of others' research or generators of their own research?
- How can teachers generate their own research?

though they may not be familiar with the teacher's context. This chapter introduces language teachers to the idea of researching their practice more formally by engaging in systematic language teacher research, using the *Language Teacher Research* series as a backdrop to the discussion.

What is Language Teacher Research?

Teacher research, or the "systematic and intentional inquiry carried out by teachers" (Cochran-Smith and Lytle, 1990: 3), is a process of actively engaging teachers in the reflection and critical evaluation of their own practices. Self-initiated professional development of this type may be necessary because teachers may have felt neglected when it comes to implementing new curricula or may have felt a lack of ownership in the materials they are using, and as a result they may have also felt a lack of self-worth or, at the very least, a feeling of lack of respect from decision makers. After all, who knows the territory best but the people who must traverse it every day, teachers and students? In fact, Freeman (1998: 6) has suggested that language teachers are best suited to carry out research in their own classrooms because they are "more insiders to their settings than researchers whose work lives are elsewhere." Freeman (1998: 6) maintained that this form of teacher research is functional because language teachers can "generate new understandings and knowledge" of their own workplaces.

This has not always been the case, however, as throughout their careers many language teachers have experienced research as something that is conducted on them by others. More often than not, the results of such research never get back to the teachers or to the institutions that hosted the outside researchers in the first place. If the results are in fact shared, then they are shared in the form of a prescription: teachers are expected to translate the results into action with the assumption that their practice will automatically improve as a result. Thus, the language teacher has often been seen as a consumer, but not a generator, of research. More recently, however, Johnson and Golombek (2002: 3) have called for language teachers to be recognized as "legitimate knowers, producers of legitimate knowledge, and as capable of constructing and sustaining their own professional practice over time." This focus firmly places the teacher in the role of generator of research knowledge. In fact, a teacher's education uniquely places that teacher in a position to provide data on classroom practice. As an interpreter of such teacher-generated research data, the teacher also becomes a stakeholder in research results (Burton 1998).

Language teacher research includes inquiries that others may refer to as *action research, practitioner inquiry, teacher inquiry, teacher self-study, teacher educator self-study*, or other labels, but does not necessarily include reflection or other terms that refer to being thoughtful about one's educational work in ways that are systematic or intentional. However, in the LTR series, teachers were specifically asked to reflect on whatever type of research they undertook by outlining a specific issue, followed by a brief literature review related to the issue, then a description of the procedures used, followed by a description of the results and a reflection about what the researcher had learned. I now provide one example from among all of the volumes, that of *Language Teacher Research in Europe*, so that you can get a feel for the main issues teachers wanted to research and how they accomplished this. Perhaps this will encourage you to read other teacher research such as can be found in the volumes of the LTR series or in some language teacher journals or magazines, such as *TESOL Quarterly*, *ELT Journal*, *Modern Language Journal*, or *Foreign Language Annals*, so that you can get more ideas on what other teachers in different contexts are reflecting on.

Because the range of topics in language teaching that teacher researchers can focus on is practically unlimited, the chapters were organized around a template to help authors and readers compare across chapters and volumes, by looking at aspects such as the research issue, background literature, procedures, results, and reflection explained as follows:

- *Issue*: The statement of the issue includes a brief description of the context and the participants.
- *Background literature*: This brief review of the literature asks authors to write only about the background literature relating to the issue being researched.
- *Procedures*: Authors document the procedures fashioned or responses made to the issue.
- *Result*: What were the results of the issue researched?
- *Reflection*: What will the researcher do now and in the future? What has the researcher learned as a result of the whole process?

Language Teacher Research in Europe

Language Teacher Research in Europe, which was edited by Simon Borg (Borg, 2006b), presents research conducted by language teachers at different levels, from high school English teachers to English language teacher educators, from different countries in Europe stretching from the United Kingdom to Turkey, and covering twelve diverse issues or topics. Table 7.1 gives a summary of the topics, the methods used in each study, the results of the studies, author reflections, and the type of setting.

The four main areas of research focused on training teachers for action research, using technology in language teaching, student attitudes to learning,

Table 7.1 Language teacher research in Europe.

Topic	Subtopic	Method/tools	Results/implications	Reflection	Setting
Training Teachers in Research	Training Teachers to Conduct Own Research	field notes (researcher)and journals (teachers)	Positive results from in-class research in own classes.	Training for in-class research good source of professional development and reflection	Public primary schools
	Student Teacher Training in Research	Course evaluations, narratives, dissertation writing, process examined	Student teachers found research training class helpful.	allow student teachers to develop researcher identities	University: graduate level
	Training in Action Research	Journal entries covering the use of action research tools, and discussion by the student teachers	Student teachers able to increase self-awareness while conducting action research.	Structured action research tools for student teachers, for them to gain confidence to conduct action research.	Primary, secondary, and post-secondary
Using Technology in Language Teaching	Internet in English for Academic Purpose (EAP) Contexts: Writing	Pre- and post-test and 400-word essay, online lessons on academic writing, questionnaires, phone interviews	Results indicated slight improvement in scores, positive feedback to lessons and use of the web.	Important to ask and listen to students' responses to teaching styles and methods.	University: undergraduate and graduate levels
	Email Journals to Foster Intercultural Learning in Foreign Language (FL) Classrooms	German EFL students paired with American students via email journals reflecting on the intercultural communication, qualitative approach	German students able to identify culturally different experiences ask for clarification from their American partner.	Journals useful not only to reflect on what learned about English culture, but also to retain information.	High school and university

Topic	Subtopic	Method/tools	Results/implications	Reflection	Setting
Student Attitudes	Student Self-Perception of Language Learning	Students' attitudes towards learning, perceptions of themselves through interviews, student narratives, self-assessment notes qualitative approach	Students successful learners when able to communicate effectively and understand the language. Students did not believe accuracy important.	Hungarians more motivated to use the L2	High school
	Motivating Students through Literature	Two classes using a variety of literature and genres, questionnaires on attitude and motivation, interviews	Most students motivated by the use and exposure to a variety of English literature including poems, stories, and other texts.	Variety of English literature allows student to play and experiment with the language and increase their vocabulary.	High school
Collaborative Learning	Learner Autonomy through Group Work	Pre- and post-test measuring grammatical, discourse, sociolinguistic, and strategic competence; questionnaires	Results showed students greatly improved across all four skills from the pre- to post-test. Students developed an awareness of communication skills through group work.	discovered that student attitudes positive	University: undergraduate level
	How Can Students Support One Another in ESP Classes	Questionnaires about learning styles and expectations, interviews	Students not part of study group ended up failing or dropping out of the course. Student support groups allowed students to review and become comfortable using English to communicate.	Students can share experiences and discuss outcomes in study groups.	University

	Levels of Student Participation in FL Classrooms	Self- assessment questionnaire about group work and willingness to interact	Self-assessment forms and heightened awareness of working in groups. Students became more aware of the different levels of participation in the group and tried to adapt to make the levels of participation equal for all students.	Important for teachers to make sure students are aware of group work interaction and to design group work carefully.	High school
Learning and Teaching Styles	Multiple Intelligences	Learning style questionnaire; a 4-step syllabus the instructor thought would “awaken, amplify, teach with/for, and transfer” the different intelligence.	Using multiple intelligences as a teaching strategy enhanced student motivation and made the material more meaningful.	Integrating different learning and teaching styles into a course helps increase student success and interest in the course.	University: undergraduate level
Language Teacher Competence	Teacher Generated Discussions in FL Contexts	The researcher recorded himself teaching and analyzed his speech to determine what types of interaction the teacher facilitates.	Simple warm up interactions at the beginning of classes are often teacher controlled and centered and that instructions and interaction during the classes are balanced between teacher and students.	Important for teachers to set up class so that students are able to use the language	University

collaborative learning, learning and teaching styles, and language teacher competence. Nearly all studies were learner-centered, meaning that the purpose of the studies was to facilitate student learning and language improvement. All studies reported positive findings in accordance to their hypothesis and research questions and had direct implications for language teaching. Most studies were qualitative studies that used interviews, journals, and questionnaires to collect data. Most research studies took place in university settings, although there were also studies conducted at the primary and secondary (elementary and high school, K–12) levels. On the whole, most of the research findings can be generalized to other language learning settings and have positive implications for second language teaching and learning.

Reflection Journal 7.3

First, write your own answers to these questions, and then find a partner or a group to discuss your findings and reflections; after these discussions in a pair or group, write a paragraph about your concluding reflections.

- Which topics in Table 7.1 do you find interesting and why?
- What role do you think the context (Europe) played (if any) in each of the studies outlined in Table 7.1?
- Comment of at least three of the reported teachers' reflections and how you think they came up with these reflections.
- Look at the topics above and choose *one* that you might want to replicate in your own setting. If you do replicate the study, it would be useful to read the original chapter from the Borg (2006b) text to make sure you replicate the procedures exactly.
- Would you use the same methods as the original study or would you change them, and if so, how and why?
- If you replicate the study, write about your findings and how different or similar they are to the original study. (You could develop such a comparative discussion in an article for a language teacher journal or magazine!)
- How would you advise other teachers to go about this type of study in the future?

Language Teacher Research Comparison Over Six Continents

Looking across the LTR studies in different parts of the world, one can consider the most common themes researched, the most common research methods used, the results, the reflections, and who the main people are that were involved in these research projects, which ask teachers at all levels to reflect on their own practice. Table 7.2 presents a summary of the entire LTR series in these terms.

Table 7.2 LTR summary table.

	Most common research theme	Methods most commonly used	Results and reflections	% of contexts as: University	Middle/ High School	Other
Europe	Improvement and development of learning methods and styles	Qualitative methods – questionnaires and interviews	Results often led to discovery of improved methods or ways of facilitating language learning or teaching Reflections often centered on the importance of language teachers to be aware of students' needs, problems, learning styles, and thoughts about learning and teaching a subsequent language.	58	34	8
Americas	Classroom practices	Qualitative methods – questionnaires, interviews, and action research projects		75	17	8
Asia	Language learning methods and styles	Qualitative methods – observation, implementing new learning tasks and methods, interviews		75	17	8
Middle East	Learning styles and problems	Qualitative methods – questionnaires and interviews		75	17	8
Africa	Writing	Qualitative methods – observation and analysis of learning tasks in the classroom		86	14	0
Australia & NZ	Culture and language learning	Qualitative methods – surveys, interviews, and implementation of courses		58	0	42

Reflection Journal 7.4

First, write your own answers to these questions, and then find a partner or a group to discuss your findings and reflections; after these discussions in a pair or group, write a paragraph about your concluding reflections.

- Looking at Table 7.2 above, what strikes you the most about the most common research theme, methods, results and reflections, and who conducts the research across these various teacher research studies?
- What do you think could be the reasons for the differing emphases reported across the LTR studies in different continents?

Table 7.2 summarizes the findings reported in the LTR series across the six continents. In the column entitled *Most common research theme*, although the range of research areas highlighted across chapters and volumes is wide, it is also interesting to note that five of the eight chapters in the Africa volume (Makalela, 2009) focus on writing development, while six of the thirteen papers in the Asia volume (Farrell, 2006) deal with greater learner independence and autonomy. Those who reported on their work in Europe (Borg, 2006b) seemed most engaged in research involving improvement and development of learning methods and styles and professional development of teachers, while teachers in Australia and New Zealand (Burns and Burton, 2008) focused on culture and language learning. The Americas research focus (McGarrell, 2007) was predominately on classroom practices as was the case for the Middle East (Coombe and Barlow, 2007). In *Methods most commonly used* column, the majority of chapters and volumes tend to use qualitative methods such as audio/video recording, classroom observations, journals, written artifacts (e.g. student written texts) questionnaires, and interviews; Europe and Australia/New Zealand stand out as most often incorporating teaching journals into their research. Some quantitative approaches can also be observed, such as the use of descriptive statistical procedures rather than experimental design. The *Percent of contexts* column demonstrates that, in each of the continents examined, university professors were among the most involved in language teacher research in this particular series of publications, with the exception of three chapters not involving participation by any university professor in the whole series. This could likely be due to the fact that academics are given more time and funding for research, and are expected to complete research regularly, whereas secondary school teachers are not (percentages were arrived at by dividing the number of each type of professional who conducted research by the total number of all authors, in each geographical area, in this series). *Results and reflections* have been combined into one column in Table 7.2 because it is apparent that each research study, despite its theme, has led to understanding and growth, which continues to drive further research. Whether conducting research for personal development, professional development, or improvement of student learning, language teacher research appears to have a global initiative: to constantly impart positive changes in a dynamic field.

Reflection Journal 7.5

First, write your own answers to these questions, and then find a partner or a group to discuss your findings and reflections; after these discussions in a pair or group, write a paragraph about your concluding reflections.

- Comment on the different research topics across all six continents. Do you think any topic that was investigated was more important than another topic, and why or why not?
- Why do you think that the majority of methods made use of qualitative procedures?
- Why do you think that university professors were much more involved in language teaching research than practicing teachers?
- How can we get more practicing teachers to become engaged in language teacher research?
- What can you surmise from the fact that the majority of the findings reportedly led to increased understanding and teacher growth?

The Future

One clear result across six continents from the language teacher research described above is that most of the language educators who are publishing their research seem to be still located in university settings. I say *publishing*, because we cannot say for sure that language teachers who teach every day in classrooms are not *researching*; it may just be that they are not publishing their findings, either thinking them not important enough to share or simply not knowing how or where to publish these findings. However, it may also be the case that they are not researching their own practices because they do not know how to do so or because they do not have the time. In fact Doan Thi Kim Khanh and Nguyen Thi Hoai An (Khanh and An, 2005) surveyed over 200 Vietnamese teachers of English to determine their attitudes toward classroom-based research and discovered that in that country, teacher research has "not been accepted as a normal part of the teaching process" (p. 4) and "ordinary teachers appear not to think that they themselves can play a key role in doing research and generating knowledge" (*ibid.*). The survey participants said that no course in their undergraduate teaching showed them how to carry out research on their own practice. So within the context of Vietnam, the lack of time (teachers may teach up to 12 hours a day) and experience, including a lack of theoretical knowledge, seem to be valid problems associated with teachers conducting research on their own practice.

I agree with Borg (2006a,b), who suggests that language teachers can, first of all, become more *aware* of the exciting possibilities of teacher research. In the past, they have been seen as having been consumers of others' research instead of being seen as themselves generators of knowledge. As Cochran-Smith and Lytle (1999: 289) have noted: "teachers and student teachers who take an inquiry stance work within inquiry communities to generate local knowledge, envision and theorize their practice, and interpret and interrogate the theory and research of others." Thus, if teachers and student teachers become more aware of and can see the possibilities of teacher research, they will become more *motivated* to engage in such research for their own professional development (Borg, 2006a). As Borg (2006a) suggests, the motivation to conduct research must be seen by individual teachers as being beneficial to their work, and they must also believe that the process of doing the research will be worthwhile. It is only when a teacher is aware and motivated that he or she can approach the "how to" aspect of teacher research, the *knowledge base and skills* associated with conducting research. In this way, teachers can make informed *choices* about how to conduct particular research that is interesting to them. Borg (2006a) also outlines six more important conditions for teachers engaging in research:

- *Mentoring* (support from a mentor);
- *Time* (time to engage in the research process);
- *Recognition* (that the classroom is recognized as a site for generating knowledge);
- *Expectations* (teachers feel research is an activity they are expected to engage in);

Reflection Journal 7.6

First, write your own answers to these questions, and then find a partner or a group to discuss your findings and reflections; after these discussions in a pair or group, write a paragraph about your concluding reflections.

- Comment on Borg's (2006a) conditions that encourage teacher research.
  Awareness:
  Motivation:
  Knowledge and skills:
  Choice:
  Mentoring:
  Time:
  Recognition:
  Expectations:
  Community:
  Dissemination potential:

- *Community* (researching in a community of like-minded professionals); and
- *Dissemination potential* (teachers need to know that their findings will be made public so others can benefit from their research).

Conclusion

In this chapter, I have outlined and discussed what language teacher professionals have reflected on in six different continents, with particular reference to some teacher research carried out in Europe. I was able to do this because I had editorial knowledge of what teachers have been researching in all of these

Chapter 7 Reflections

First, write your own answers to these questions, and then find a partner or a group to discuss your findings and reflections; after these discussions in a pair or group, write a paragraph about your concluding reflections.

- Why should language teachers on the front lines bother to conduct research on their own practices?
- What to you is the point about becoming generators of research rather than consumers of others' research?
- Lorense (1994: 1) states that "historically, teachers have never been an important source of information for educational change." What do you think of this statement?
- Mazzillo (1995: 45) says, "When the idea [of doing classroom research] was first introduced to me, I was sceptical." Why might a teacher have this attitude to classroom research?
- Allwright (1997) suggests that lack of support is another reason making teachers reluctant to do classroom research. How can you overcome this?
- Hopkins (2002) maintains that classroom research is an extra burden that introduces more work and responsibilities for many teachers. What do you think? What gains can you get from conducting classroom research?
- What do you think is the biggest obstacle to you conducting research in your own classroom? How can you overcome this?
- Belanger (1992: 17) highlights a main constraint which keeps teachers from doing classroom research: time. How can you overcome this constraint?
- In contrast to the above comment, Gunn (2003: 7) says that "through researching what puzzles me about my classroom...using pedagogical activities that I am comfortable with and involving my students, I now have a better understanding of why things happen in my class the way they do." What do you think of this statement?

different locations. The idea of the TESOL series was not to pad researchers' bookshelves, but to add to the knowledge of what practicing teachers actually consider important in their own real classrooms around the world. I have outlined and briefly discussed each continent's findings with the hope that the reader will look into topics from these studies that interest him or her and even replicate some of the studies within his/her own context.

The Last Word on Reflection?

Reflection may not be for every teacher; one's desire and ability to reflect is probably also linked to one's psychological and emotional states at any given time. In other words, teachers need to be ready to reflect, as the process of reflection may involve some feeling of unease. Reflecting is something like someone waking you up in the middle of the night when you don't want to wake up because you are comfortable, and why should you anyway. But it is worth asking yourself whether you have slipped into a comfortable routine in which the routine is driving your teaching rather than any conscious reflection on what you are actually doing in the classroom? Are you now also suggesting that you can do what you have always done with the idea that all of your students are the same and it mostly works?

Even if teachers find themselves working at the level of routine action, I will bet they also feel that something is missing in their professional lives. However, just as we do not want to be woken in the middle of the night because we are comfortable, I suggest that this level of comfort will lead to eventual burnout because we are not questioning our routine acts of teaching and its impact on our students' learning. As Dewey (1933: 17) noted, reflection is a form of freedom from routine behavior because "reflection emancipates us from merely impulsive and merely routine activity; it enables us to direct our activities with foresight and to plan according to ends-in-view or purposes of which we are aware, to act in deliberate and intentional fashion, to know what we are about when we act."

Throughout this book, I have encouraged language teachers to engage in systematic reflective practice mainly through the medium of writing so that they can become more aware of their beliefs and teaching routines, on the assumption that this would lead to professional development and growth as a teaching professional. I have used my own teaching career as an example of how writing has helped me reflect from my early days as an English language teacher in Korea to my doctoral dissertation writing during my graduate student experiences in the United States and my later development as a language teacher educator. I find the act of writing necessary for me as I reflect because it slows down my thoughts and allows me to see them when I put them on a page or screen. Then I can begin to make more sense of my reflections. I also realize that writing may not be for everybody, but I hope that all teachers (from novice to the most experienced) who take the time to read this book and to work through its reflective activities will be able to get some ideas about how to move beyond routine in their work, even if they do not want to write about it. We engage in reflective practice not because we want to teach our lessons better (although this is a good reason), but because we want to teach our students better.

References

Allwright, Dick (1997) Quality and sustainability in teacher-research. *TESOL Quarterly* 31: 368–70.

Bailey, Kathleen M. (1990) The use of diary studies in teacher education programs. In Jack C. Richards and David Nunan (eds.) *Second Language Teacher Education* 215–26. New York: Cambridge University Press.

Bailey, Kathleen M. (2001) Action research, teacher research, and classroom research in language teaching. In Marianne Celce-Murcia (ed.) *Teaching English as a Second or Foreign language* (3rd edition) 489–98. Boston, Massachusetts: Heinle and Heinle.

Bailey, Kathleen M., Curtis, Andy and Nunan, David (2001) *Pursuing Professional Development: The Self as Source*. Boston: Heinle and Heinle.

Belanger, Joe (1992) Teacher research as a lifelong experiment. *English Journal* 81: 16–23.

Belbin, R. Meredith (1993) *Team Roles at Work*. Oxford: Butterfield-Heinemann.

Bliss, Leonard B., and Reck, Una M. (1991) *PROFILE: An Instrument for Gathering Data in Teacher Socialization Studies* (ERIC Document Reproduction Service No. 330 662).

Borg, Simon (2006a) Conditions for teacher research. *English Teaching Forum* 4: 22–7.

Borg, Simon (ed.) (2006b) *Language Teacher Research in Europe*. Alexandria, Virginia: TESOL.

Brock, Mark, Yu, Bart and Wong, Mabel (1992) "Journalling" together: Collaborative diary-keeping and teacher development. In John Flowerdew, Mark Brock, and Sophie Hsia (eds.) *Perspectives on Second Language Teacher Development*, 295–307. Hong Kong: City University of Hong Kong.

Brookfield, Stephen D. (1990) *The Skillful Teacher: On Technique, Trust and Responsiveness in the Classroom*. San Francisco: Jossey-Bass.

Brumfit, Christopher J. and Johnson, Kerrie (eds.) (1979) *The Communicative Approach to Language Teaching*. Oxford: Oxford University Press.

Bullough, Robert V., Jr. and Baughman, K. (1993) Continuity and change in teacher development: A first year teacher after five years. *Journal of Teacher Education* 44: 86–95.

Burns, Anne (1999) *Collaborative Action Research for English Language Teachers*. Cambridge: Cambridge University Press.

Burns, Anne, and Burton, Jill (eds.) (2008) *Language Teacher Research in Australia and New Zealand*. Alexandria, Virginia: TESOL.

Burton, Jill (1998) A cross-case analysis of teacher involvement in TESOL research. *TESOL Quarterly* 32: 419–46.

Burton, Jill (2005) The importance of teachers writing on TESOL. *TESL-EJ* 9(2): 1–18.

Carew, Jean and Lightfoot, Sara L. (1979) *Beyond Bias: Perspectives on Classrooms.* Cambridge, Massachusetts: Harvard University Press.

Clarke, David J. and Hollingsworth, Hilary (2002) Elaborating a model of teacher professional growth *Teaching and Teacher Education* 18(8): 947–67.

Cochran-Smith, Marilyn and Lytle, Susan L. (1999) The teacher research movement: A decade later. *Educational Researcher* 28: 7, 15–25.

Coombe, Christine and Barlow, Lisa (eds.) (2007) *Language Teacher Research in the Middle East*. Alexandria, Virginia: TESOL.

Connelly, F. Michael and Clandinin, D. Jean (1990) Stories of experience and narrative inquiry. *Educational Researcher* 19: 2–14.

Cortazzi, Martin (1994) Narrative analysis. *Language Teacher* 27: 157–70.

Curran, Charles A. (1972) *Counselling-Learning: A Whole-Person Model for Education.* New York: Grune and Stratton.

Devi, Nandprasar Sushila (2002) Study of six primary school English language teachers as they reflect on their teaching of reading. Unpublished M.A. thesis. National Institute of Education, Singapore.

Dewey, John (1933) *How We Think.* Madison, Wisconsin: University of Wisconsin Press.

Dewey, John (1938) *Experience and Education*, New York: Collier Books.

Dutra, Deise P. and Mello, Heliana (2008) Self-observation and reconceptualisation through narratives and reflective practice. In Paula Kalaja, Vera Menezes and Ana Maria F. Barcelos (eds.) *Narratives of Learning and Teaching EFL* 49–63. Basingstoke: Palgrave Macmillan.

Elbow, Peter (1981) *Writing With Power.* New York: Oxford University Press.

Eisenman, Gordon and Thornton, Holly (1999) Telementoring: Helping new teachers through the first year. *THE. Journal* 26: 79–82.

Evans, Linda (2002) What is teacher development? *Oxford Review of Education* 28: 123–37.

Fanselow, John F. (1987) *Breaking Rules*. New York: Longman.

Fanselow, John F. (1988) "Let's see": Contrasting conversations about teaching. *TESOL Quarterly* 22: 113–20.

Farrell, Thomas S. C. (1996) A qualitative study of a group of English as a foreign language teachers in Korea as they reflect on their work. *Dissertation Abstracts International* 57: 3005A (UMI No. 9636926).

Farrell, Thomas S. C. (1998) Communicating with colleagues of a different culture. In Jack C. Richards (ed.) *Teaching in Action: Case Studies from Second Language Classrooms* 125–8. Alexandria, Virginia: TESOL.

Farrell, Thomas S. C. (1999) The reflective assignment: Unlocking pre-service English teachers' beliefs on grammar teaching. *RELC Journal* 30: 1–17.

Farrell, Thomas S. C. (2004) *Reflective Practice in Action.* Thousand Oaks, California: Corwin Press.

Farrell, Thomas S. C. (2006) *Language Teacher Research in Asia.* Alexandria, Virginia: TESOL.

Farrell, Thomas S. C. (2007) *Reflective Language Teaching: From Research to Practice.* London: Continuum Press.

Farrell, Thomas S. C. (ed.) (2008a) *Novice Language Teachers: Insights and Perspectives for the First Year*. London: Equinox.

Farrell, Thomas S. C. (2008b) Reflective practice in the professional development of teachers of adult English language learners. *CAELA Network Brief*, October 2008: 1–4. Washington, D.C.: Center for Applied Linguistics.

Farrell, Thomas S. C. (2009) The novice teacher. In Anne Burns and Jack C. Richards (eds.) *The Cambridge Guide to Language Teacher Education*. New York: Cambridge University Press.

Feiman-Nemser, Sharon and Floden, Robert E. (1986) The cultures of teaching. In Merlin C. Wittrock (ed.) *Handbook of Research on Teaching* (3rd edition) 505–25. New York: Macmillan.

Forster, E. M. (1966/1927) *Aspects of the Novel*. Harmondsworth: Penguin (originally published 1927).

Fox, Dennis (1983) Personal theories of teaching. *Studies in Higher Education* 8(2): 151–63.

Freeman, Donald (1993) Renaming experience/reconstructing practice: Developing new understandings of teaching. *Teaching and Teacher Education* 9 (5/6): 485–497.

Freeman, Donald (1998) How to see: The challenges of integrating teaching and research in your own classroom. *The English Connection* 2: 6–8.

Freeman, Donald and Richards, Jack C. (1993) Conceptions of teaching and the education of second language teachers. *TESOL Quarterly* 27: 193–216.

Fullan, Michael (1991) *The New Meaning of Educational Change*. New York: Teachers College Press.

Gattegno, Caleb (1972) *Teaching Foreign Languages in Schools: The Silent Way*. New York: Educational Solutions.

Garro, Linda C. and Mattingly, Cheryl (2000) Narrative as construct and construction. In Linda C. Garro and Cheryl Mattingly (eds.) *Narrative and the Cultural Construction of Illness and Healing* 1–49. Berkeley: University of California Press.

Gebhard, Jerry G. (1992) Awareness of teaching: Approaches, benefits, tasks. *English Teaching Forum* 30(4): 2–7.

Golombek, Paula R. and Johnson, Karen E. (2004) Narrative inquiry as a mediational space: Examining cognitive and emotional dissonance in second language teachers' development. Teachers and teaching: *Theory and Practice* 10: 307–27.

Gow, Lyn, Kember, David and McKay, Jan (1996) Improving student learning through action research into teaching. In David A. Watkins and John B. Biggs (eds.) *The Chinese Learner: Cultural, Psychological and Contextual Influences* 243–65. Hong Kong: Comparative Education Research Centre (CERC) & Australian Council of Educational Research (ACER).

Gunn, Cindy L. (2003) Exploratory practice: A research technique for teachers. *Perspectives* 11(1): 4–9.

Guskey, Thomas R. (2000) *Evaluating Professional Development*. Thousand Oaks, California: Corwin Press.

Hatton, Neville and Smith, David (1995) Reflection in teacher education: Towards definition and implementation. *Teaching and Teacher Education* 11: 33–9.

Head, Katie, and Taylor, Pauline (1997) *Readings in Teacher Development*. London: Heinemann.

Ho, Belinda and Richards, Jack C. (1993) Reflective thinking through teacher journal writing: Myths and realities. *Prospect* 8(3): 7–24.

Holly, Mary Louise (1989) *Writing to Grow. Keeping a Personal-Professional Journal*. Portsmouth, New Hampshire: Heinemann.

Hopkins, David (2002) *A Teacher's Guide to Classroom Research* (3rd edition). Philadelphia: Open University Press.

Hornberger, Nancy H. (1994) Ethnography. *TESOL Quarterly* 28: 688–90.

Huberman, Michael A. (1993) *The Lives of Teachers. New York:* Teachers *College Press.*

Hunt, David (1980) How to be your own best theorist. *Theory into Practice* 19: 287–93.

Hymes, Dell H. (1966) Two types of linguistic relativity. In W. Bright (ed.) *Sociolinguistics* 114–58. The Hague: Mouton.

Jalongo, Mary R. and Isenberg, Joan P. (1995) *Teachers' Stories: From Personal Narrative to Professional Insight.* San Francisco: Jossey Bass Publishers.

Jarvis, Jennifer (1996) Using diaries for teacher refection on in-service courses. In Tricia Hedge and Norman Whitney (eds.) *Power, Pedagogy and Practice* 307–23). Oxford: Oxford University Press.

Jersild, Arthur (1955) *When Teachers Face Themselves.* New York: Teachers College Press.

Johnson, Karen E. and Golombek, Paula R. (2002) *Teacher's Narrative Inquiry as Professional Development*. New York: Cambridge University Press.

Kagan, Donna M. (1992) Professional growth among pre-service and beginning teachers. *Review of Educational Research* 64: 129–69.

Khanh, Doan T. K. and An, Nguyen T. H. (2005) Teachers' attitudes to classroom research in Vietnam. *Teacher's Edition* 18: 4–7.

Knezedivc, Borbas (2001) Action research. *IATEFL Teacher Development SIG Newsletter* 1: 10–12.

Lange, Dale (1990) A blueprint for a teacher development program. In Jack C. Richards and David Nunan (eds.) *Second Language Teacher Education* 245–68. New York: Cambridge University Press.

Krashen, Stephen D. (1981) *Second Language Acquisition and Second Language Learning.* Oxford: Pergamon.

Krashen, Stephen D. (1982) *Principles and Practice in Second Language Acquisition.* Oxford: Pergamon.

Krashen, Stephen D. (1985) *The Input Hypothesis: Issues and Implications*. New York: Longman.

Lakoff, George and Johnson, Mark (1980) *Metaphors We Live By*. Chicago: University of Chicago Press.

Lofland, John and Lofland, Lyn (1984) *Analyzing Local Settings: A Quick Guide to Qualitative Observation and Analysis*. Belmont, California: Woodsworth.

Lorense, Mary B. (1994) Action research: Are teachers finding their voice? *The Elementary School Journal* 95(1): 1–10.

Lortie, Donald (1975) *Schoolteacher: A Sociological Study.* Chicago: University of Chicago Press.

Makalela, Leketi (2009) *Language Teacher in AFRICA*. Alexandria, Virginia: TESOL.

Malderez, Angi and Bodoczky, Caroline (1999) *Mentor Courses: A Resource Book for Teacher-Trainers.* Cambridge: Cambridge University Press.

Mann, Steve (2005) The language teacher's development. *Language Teaching* 38: 103–18.

Mason, John (2002) *Researching Your Own Practice: The Discipline of Noticing*. New York: Routledge.

Maynard, Trisha and Furlong, John (1995) Learning to teach and models of mentoring. In Trevor Kerry and Ann Shelton Mayes (eds.) *Issues in Mentoring* 10–24. London: Routledge.

Mazzillo, Tania M. (1995) On becoming a researcher. *TESOL Journal* 4(1): 45–6.

McCabe, Anne (2002) A wellspring for development. In Julian Edge (ed.) *Continuing Professional Development* 82–96. Whitstable, UK: IATEFL Publications.

McDonough, Jo (1994) A teacher looks at teachers' diaries, *English Language Teaching Journal* 18: 57–65.

McGarrell, Hedy (1997) *Language Teacher Research in the Americas.* Alexandria, Virginia: TESOL.

Miccoli, Laura (2006) Brazilian EFL Teachers' Experiences in Public and Private Schools: Different Contexts with Similar Challenges. In Paula Kalaja, Vera Menezes, Ana Maria F. Barcelos (eds.) *Narratives of Learning and Teaching EFL* 64–82. London: Palgrave Macmillan.

Moon, Jennifer (2006) *Learning Journals: A Handbook for Academics, Students and Professional Development*. London: Routledge.

Nias, Jennifer (1987) Learning from difference: A collegial approach to change. In John Smyth (ed.) *Educating Teachers: Changing the Nature of Pedagogical Knowledge* 137–52. Barcombe, UK: Falmer Press.

Olshtain, Elite and Kupferberg, Irit (1998) Reflective-narrative discourse of FL teachers exhibits professional knowledge. *Language Teaching Research* 2: 185–202.

Osterman, Karen F. and Kottkamp, Robert B. (1993). *Reflective Practice for Educators: Improving Schooling through Professional Development.* Thousand Oaks, California: Corwin Press.

Palmer, Peter J. (1998) *The Courage to Teach.* San Francisco: Jossey-Bass.

Peyton, Joy Kreeft and Reed, Leslee (1990). *Dialogue Journal Writing with Nonnative English Speakers: A Handbook for Teachers*. Alexandria, Virginia: TESOL.

Richards, Jack C. (1990) Beyond training: Approaches to teacher education in language teaching. *The Language Teacher* 14: 3–8.

Richards, Jack C. and Farrell, Thomas S. C. (2005) *Professional Development for Language Teachers*. New York: Cambridge University Press.

Richards, Jack C. and Farrell, Thomas S. C. (2011) *Practice Teaching: A Reflective Approach.* New York: Cambridge University Press.

Richards, Jack C. and Lockhart, Charles (1994) *Reflective Teaching*. New York: Cambridge University Press.

Richards, Jack C. and Pennington, Martha C. (1998) The first year of teaching. In Jack C. Richards (ed.) *Beyond Training* 173–90. New York: Cambridge University Press.

Richardson, Laurel and St. Pierre, Elizabeth (1994) Writing: A method of inquiry. In Norman Denzin and Yvonna Lincoln (eds.) *Handbook of Qualitative Research* (3rd edition) 955–78. London: Sage. Cited in Moon (2006).

Seow, Anthony (2002) The writing process and process writing. In Jack C. Richards and Willie A. Reynanda (eds.) *Methodology in Language Teaching: An Anthology of Current Practice* 315–20. Cambridge: Cambridge University Press.

Skinner, Barbara (2002) Moving on: From training course to workplace. *ELT Journal* 56 (3): 267–72.

Smith, Christine, Hofer, Judy, Gillespie, Marilyn, Solomon, Marla and Rowe, Karen (2003) *How Teachers Change: A Study of Professional Development in Adult Education* (Report No. 25a). Cambridge, Massachusetts: National Center for the Study of Adult Learning and Literacy.

Stanley, Liz (1992) *The Auto/Biographical I*. Manchester: Manchester University Press.

Stevick, Earl W. (1980) *Teaching Languages: A Way and Ways*. Rowley, Massachusetts: Newbury House.

Tarone, Elaine and Allwright, Dick (2005) Second language teacher learning and student second language learning: Shaping the knowledge base. In Diane J. Tedick (ed.) *Second Language Teacher Education* 5–23. Mahwah, New Jersey: Lawrence Erlbaum.

Tedick, Diane J. (ed.) (2005) *Second Language Teacher Education: International Perspectives*. Mahwah, New Jersey: Lawrence Erlbaum Associates.

Tripp, David (1993) *Critical Incidents in Teaching*. London: Routledge.

Tsui, Amy B. M. (1995) *Introducing Classroom Interaction*. London: Penguin.

Underhill, Adrian (1999) Continuous teacher development. *IATEFL Issues* 149: 14–18.

Valli, Linda (1997) Listening to other voices: A description of teacher reflection in the United States. *Peabody Journal of Education* 72: 67–88.

Varah, Leonard J., Theune, Warren S. and Parker, Linda (1986) Beginning teachers: Sink or swim? *Journal of Teacher Education* 37: 30–33.

Veenman, Simon (1984) Perceived problems of beginning teachers. *Review of Educational Research* 54: 143–78.

Wallace, Michael J. (1991) *Teacher Training: A Reflective Approach*. Cambridge: Cambridge University Press.

Wallace, Michael J. and Woolger, David (1991) Improving the ELT supervisory dialogue: The Sri Lanka experience. *ELT Journal* 45: 320–27.

Williams, Anne, Prestage, Stephanie and Bedward, Julie (2001) Individualism to collaboration: The significance of teacher culture to the induction of newly qualified teachers. *Journal of Education for Teaching* 27(3): 253–-67.

Index

www.ingramcontent.com/pod-product-compliance
Lightning Source LLC
LaVergne TN
LVHW010448080826
844660LV00027B/1236